POLITICAL BETRAYAL:
HOW HAUGHEY ACQUIRED €70M

# POLITICAL BETRAYAL

## HOW CHARLES HAUGHEY ACQUIRED €70M

### KEVIN O'CONNOR

Copyright © Kevin O'Connor 2021
ISBN: 9798773312765

## Biographical note

Operating behind the scenes in the Dáil for nearly thirty years as Parliamentary Correspondent for the *Sunday Independent*, Limerick city born Kevin O Connor for a long time monitored the brilliant career of Charles J. Haughey, one of the most astute politicians to grace Leinster House.

His best seller *Sweetie* disclosed that Haughey spent €27,000 a month on wining, dining, and holidays for his mistress, journalist Terry Keane. That book forced gossip columnist Keane to come out in the open after twenty-seven years and reveal her passionate affair with the former Taoiseach.

Kevin O'Connor's popular inside politics column "Backchat" in the *Sunday Independent* revealed many world exclusives. An RTÉ television programme called the "Roscommon File", based on a story he had written, provided a detailed catalogue of abuses of power by Haughey's Justice Minister, Sean Doherty. That dramatic story helped to further undermine that scandal-ridden Haughey government.

In 1992, when Albert Reynolds became Taoiseach, Kevin O'Connor presented a paper to him on the importance of the Irish Diaspora and how the Government could tap into the forty-four million Irish – in particular the 40% of American chief executives – who are of Irish origin. Consequently, Reynolds appointed an international marketing committee to act as a sounding board for ideas and help to market Ireland internationally. Out of that committee came the "Gathering" concept in 2013, resulting in eight million people coming to Ireland, contributing some €3.64 billion to the economy.

# CONTENTS

Biographical note      v

Acknowledgments      ix

## INTRODUCTION      1

## THE PHILANDERER      9
• THE DÁIL DON JUAN • A DUBLIN DALLIANCE • A LOUIS VUITTON HANDBAG • ADVICE TO A GARDA • WHO WAS JANE'S FATHER? • THE NAKED LADY • THE NIGHT THE CHANDELIERS SHOOK • A SPECIAL NIGHT • TRIPS ABROAD • TERRY IN HOSPITAL • TERRY'S BETRAYAL OF CHARLIE

## HAUGHEY AND NORTHERN IRELAND      31
• HEROES OF THE ARMS CRISIS • BOLAND ON THE ARMS CRISIS • THE ARMY'S SECRET POLICY • HAUGHEY'S PEACE MOVES • BOMB SCARE • WAS HAUGHEY AN IRA SPY? • DÁIL SPY

## THE BULLY BOY      57
• HAUGHEY'S TAKE ON POLITICS • HAUGHEY AND THE SECRET COURTS • THE POLITICS OF SURVIVAL • SENATOR TOLD TO JUMP • OFFICIAL HUMILIATED • CLASH WITH LIAM LAWLOR • RTÉ ENCOUNTER • GEMMA'S 'BRUSH' WITH HAUGHEY • A POLITICAL BURIAL • THREATS TO A GARDA AND AN ARMY OFFICER

## HOW IT ALL CAME TO AN END      83
• DR JOHN OUT-MANOEUVRES HAUGHEY • TWIN ATTACK TO UNSEAT HAUGHEY • FINAL DAYS AS TAOISEACH • HIGH DRAMA ON THE 17TH FLOOR • HOW MY STORY ABOUT DOHERTY WAS SPIKED • GUESS WHO TAPPED THE GOVERNMENT? • FIANNA FÁIL IN AMERICA

## MONEY MATTERS  117
• THE REAL STORY OF THE CARYSFORT DEAL • MYSTERY OF TANGLED FINANCES • REGULAR VISITORS TO KINSEALY • A FINANCIAL KILLING • HIS BIGGEST EARNER • TRIBUNALS LEAVE REPUTATION IN TATTERS • AN UNSOLVED MYSTERY • FOOD FAVOURS

## ON THE FUNNY SIDE  137
• A PERSONAL ENCOUNTER • MISTAKEN IDENTITY • UNEASY RELATIONS WITH THE MEDIA • A THATCHER MOMENT • HAUGHEY'S VIEW OF GANGSTERS • NUCLEAR MISSILES IN WICKLOW • NEW WINE INTO OLD • THE MEDJUGORJE TOUCH • A SACKING MATTER

## THE HAUGHEY LEGACY: THE GOOD, THE BAD, AND THE UGLY  151
• HIS GREATEST SERVICE • INEXPENSIVE GESTURES • DEV'S FOREBODING • THE LENIHAN FUND • HAUGHEY'S GENEROSITY TO CONSTITUENTS • A CULTURE OF CORRUPTION

Index  165

## Acknowledgments

I would like to acknowledge the contributions of many who helped make this difficult adventure possible.

First, there is my chief researcher, my partner Anne, whose carefully prepared research and invaluable advice ensured the eventual launch of *Political Betrayal*.

The project, of course, could never have materialised without the most important people of all – my excellent contacts in the security and political arena who gave me superb information, often at considerable risk to their own position and reputation.

Finally, I wish to devote the book to my late brother, Fr Dermot O Connor, C.SS.r, a dedicated Redemptorist missionary in Brazil, who died in August 2021 after a long illness.

# INTRODUCTION

# INTRODUCTION

The reaction to the launch of Sweetie, my best-selling book that examined the career of former Taoiseach Charles Haughey and broke the story of his affair with journalist Terry Keane, could not have been more dramatic or – for a few weeks – more frightening.

Firstly, I learned that in order to maintain maximum pressure on me, Haughey and Keane made a personal call to Tony O'Reilly, the then proprietor of Independent Newspapers, where I worked, to stop the publication. To his credit, O'Reilly never made any representations to me. He knew me well enough to know that it would have been a waste of his valuable time.

And then, three weeks before the launch of the book, a close associate of Seamus Brennan, the former Minister for Transport, threatened me in a Dublin hotel. I was having a brief meeting with the late Des O'Malley, the leader of the Progressive Democrats, when Brennan's friend called me aside. He surprised me when he said: "I just want to tell you, if you come out with that book on Haughey, at least four Ministers plan to get you."

Looking him straight in the eyes, I immediately countered: "Throughout my career, I have been threatened at various times. It has never worked, it won't work now, and you can tell that to your paymasters".

Despite my immediate dismissal of his threat, I took it seriously. For the next six weeks, I engaged a former British paratrooper, the friend of a friend, to watch our back at our isolated home in Roundwood, Co. Wicklow.

Within a week, two gunmen arrived at our home. I was on my way home with the paratrooper when my partner, Anne, called. I could hear our Rottweiler dog barking fiercely in the kitchen and Anne interrupted our call to see what was happening. I could hear her shouting, but I still did not know the problem.

Anne came back to the phone to tell me that a gunman, crouched over a wheelie bin, had pointed a gun at her from ten yards away, as the dog was snarling to attack him. She had bravely opened the kitchen door four inches and shouted at the gunman: "If you are not off this property in 10 seconds, I will leave the dog out".

The gunman, who dropped a badge from his pocket in fright, was gone in five seconds and joined another man who was sitting in a blue Ford Mondeo. He appeared to be the getaway driver parked in our long front driveway.

Anne told me that they drove towards Roundwood, then turned around just 200 metres from our home and sped towards Bray and the Sugar Loaf – just as I was approaching the long hill at the Sugar Loaf. Five minutes later, the gunmen passed me in their blue Mondeo, driving with the full lights on at ninety miles per hour at least. I could not obtain the number plate.

Gardaí from Harcourt Street visited us the next day, and Anne, who is an artist, drew a graphic picture of the gunman. We both made detailed statements. The gardaí said they would get back to us.

A week later, Anne and I saw what appeared to be the two gunmen at the filling station at Kilmacanogue on the N11– just ten minutes from our house. They were in the front seat of a blue Mondeo… which appeared to be a Garda car.

Our problems were not over. A couple of days later, Anne was on her own in our house and was alerted by the dog barking. When she investigated the problem, she saw a bright light at the back of the house. The whole half of the kerosene tank was alight, with the kerosene dripping from the side of the tank. Anne, who had no time to call the fire brigade, grabbed the garden hose to douse the flames. The emergency was over in a few minutes.

As the kerosene tank was being replaced the next day, the engineer told us we were extremely fortunate because the system was within seconds of blowing through the fuel lines under the property. The whole house was within seconds of exploding, he said.

A couple of days later, Anne was driving out of her office in Blessington when she noticed a van on her tail. As she crossed the bridge on the Blessington Lakes, the van was still following. She proceeded along the lakeside road, heading towards the Sally Gap, the van remaining behind her. A few moments later, she pulled into the side of the road, and the van had no option but to overtake her. She followed the van and the driver tried to block her on a few occasions. At the Sally Gap crossroads, an isolated boggy area, she telephoned me, advised what had happened, and gave the registration number and description of the vehicle.

A few moments later, Wicklow gardaí were able to tell me that the van had been stolen from the Dart Station in Bray that morning. The gardaí also had vital information on the badge we found on our driveway. They told us it was a staff badge belonging to someone called "Robert", who had worked in Mount Juliet Golf Club and lived in Kilkenny. They intended to question him in more detail, but they learned he had re-located to the U.K. There was no follow-up.

In all these incidents, we are talking attempted murder: what could have been a fatal arson attack and an attempt to intimidate my partner Anne by driving in a reckless and dangerous fashion over the Sally Gap.

Six years later, I sent a letter to the Chief Superintendent for the Wicklow-Wexford area, M.R. Murphy, requesting the result of the garda investigation by several Garda stations, including Harcourt Street detectives, Roundwood, Bray, Wicklow, and Wexford. All I received was an acknowledgment.

Three months later, I sent another letter to Supt. Murphy. This time I received an acknowledgment from Chief Supt. Roche, saying my letter had been passed to the Divisional Officer in Bray. Another letter three months later from me to Murphy who said he had sent it to the District Officer in Wicklow and advised him to ensure that the matter is addressed "as a matter of urgency".

With nothing happening for five years and the Gardaí failing in their duty to keep us informed, I wrote to the then Ombudsman, Emily O'Reilly, who agreed to send my file to the Garda Ombudsman.

That was in July 2010.

The Ombudsman subsequently agreed that my complaints were admissible. Supt. Eamonn Keogh from Baltinglass, Co Wicklow, was in charge of our case. He was later transferred to the Fraud Squad.

The upshot of his investigation was that files in relation to the matter are all missing from Hardcourt Street, Roundwood, Bray, Wicklow and Wexford. How convenient! I can understand one file being missing, but five is downright suspicious, inexcusable and unbelievable.

Also, hard evidence was submitted to the local garda station at Roundwood. This was mislaid. The Garda Ombudsman's office decided to discontinue the investigation in March 2014. They stated that Supt. Keogh "has exhausted all avenues available to him to trace the investigation files and the correspondence referred to in your complaint without success".

The letter added: "While it may not be considered satisfactory that files of this nature can be mislaid, this is the case and it was on that basis that GSOC decided to discontinue the investigation of your complaint in accordance with s.93 (1) of the Garda Síochána Act, 2005 (the Act) as further investigation was not considered necessary or practicable".

With this unacceptable situation, I was more determined to fully investigate unproven stories I had heard about Charles Haughey, who himself knew a thing or two about missing files. He was a former Minister for Justice and was acting Minister for Justice during the terms of Maire Geoghegan-Quinn, Padraig Flynn, and the late Sean Doherty. That allowed him to send for any file he wished to see. During my investigations, I became aware that he disposed of many files which were potentially embarrassing to him.

Over the past few years, I have been busy working on Political Betrayal, which is a collection of stories and investigations on Haughey and some on Terry Keane. Haughey trousered up to €70 million from big business while in office, betrayed the public trust and the nation and reaped a huge dividend for his efforts for himself.

# INTRODUCTION

Terry Keane betrayed Haughey by revealing on the "Late Late Show" her affair of twenty-seven years with the former Taoiseach –and collecting almost €300,000 from various newspapers for her troubles.

And the late Michael Hand, my former editor in the *Sunday Independent*, betrayed the noble and honourable profession of journalism by not using my world exclusive in 1982 on former Minister for Justice, the late Sean Doherty who was guilty of widespread abuse of power in his own constituency of Roscommon and throughout the country.

The newspaper's lawyers cleared the story to run when they saw I had five garda statements backing up the controversial story. But Hand bowed to Fianna Fáil pressure at that time and dropped the story. I had no other option but to give the piece to RTÉ who called it "The Roscommon File". That was after a controversial phone call to Tony O'Reilly, who was at his home in Pittsburgh, USA. Being a whistle blower in the Indo at that time was not a pleasant task or experience, particularly after a three-week suspension.

Enjoy *Political Betrayal*!

# THE PHILANDERER

## THE DÁIL DON JUAN

Throughout his career in the Dáil, Haughey was a notorious womaniser. And the problem for him was that his dalliances got him into serious physical rows several times, the most serious of which came in April 1970 when he was Minister for Finance.

He was due to deliver the Budget on Wednesday, April 22, 1970, but that morning Taoiseach Jack Lynch was told that Haughey had been injured in a riding accident and would not be able to do so.

Within days, a rumour began to circulate – that he had been beaten up in a pub after being caught with a young girl in *flagrante delicto* by her father and brother.

It was the wish of Lynch and the powerful Secretary of the Department of Justice, Peter Berry, that there would be no Garda investigation of any of the rumours.

In his memoirs, Berry said the Garda Commissioner telephoned him to say Haughey had fallen from a horse and was in the Mater. Berry then informed Lynch, who had already heard it from another source.

Berry wrote: "Later, the commissioner phoned me again to say the rumour was circulating that Haughey's accident had occurred on a licensed premises the previous night. When I informed the Taoiseach of the rumour, as reported by the commissioner, he said: 'Oh no, not that, too.'

"He went on to agree there should be no police inquiries. He was emphatic on that. I conveyed the Taoiseach's view to the commissioner."

Berry was a powerful figure. However, he did not reckon with another forceful personality with deep convictions – the new Minister for Justice, Des O'Malley, who ordered a Garda investigation into the incident despite Berry's protests.

Three weeks later, Peter Berry and the Garda superintendent from the Clonee area of north Meath reported to O'Malley's office.

*The Grasshopper Inn in Co. Meath, where, according to a Garda report, Haughey was beaten up by the angry son and father of a young girl.*

They told him that Haughey was "in a *flagrante delicto* situation" in the upstairs bedroom of the Grasshopper Inn pub in Clonlee when surprised by the young girl's father and brother. Armed with an iron bar, they broke up chairs and hit Haughey around the head and shoulders, giving him an "unmerciful hiding" that almost killed him. The incident happened between 11 and 11.30 the night before the budget.

Writing about the incident in his memoirs, Des O'Malley said: "The official story stated that he was the victim of a horse-riding accident that morning at Kinsealy, which had rendered him unconscious. However, doubt was immediately cast upon that version of events; rumours began to circulate that Haughey had actually been the victim of a violent assault, carried out by persons unknown upon the discovery of a personal indiscretion.

"Indeed, this was the story related to me by Peter Berry some weeks after I was appointed Minister for Justice. He, in turn, had been informed by the Gardaí."

Later, in a phone call, Des O'Malley told me that the Gardaí originally informed him about the Grasshopper Inn incident and what happened Haughey. He was never given the name of the girl involved or the names of her brother and father. Berry and the Garda superintendent also asked for guidance: should they prosecute the father and son for inflicting substantial injuries on Haughey?

O'Malley knew that his late uncle – the great Donogh O'Malley – was a close friend of Haughey's. He considered the fact that the former Minister for Finance was now a broken man, sacked from the Government and beginning his political wilderness. "No", said Des O'Malley, "Mr Haughey has suffered enough."

O'Malley could have been accused of negligence for not charging the father and son with attempted murder. Similarly, he was remiss in not ordering an investigation into the age of the girl.

Apparently, there was no police investigation on the girl involved. All the evidence was that she was very young. Could she have been sexually exploited? Could Haughey have been a sexual predator… even a paedophile? In the Ireland of the squinting windows of 1970, Haughey's career would have been over had the truth been revealed at that time by O'Malley. Without a doubt, O'Malley did Haughey a big favour, saved his career and participated in a 50-year cover-up.

In his biography of Jack Lynch, Dermot Keogh wrote: "Haughey did not report to the Department of Finance on the day of the budget, Wednesday, 22 April, as he had been badly beaten up earlier that morning in a public house in unclear circumstances and for unconfirmed reasons. His injuries were so severe - an iron bar having been used by his attacker or attackers – that he had been admitted as an emergency case to the Mater Hospital."

On Monday, May 11, the media were told in a special press conference organised by Haughey's legal advisor, solicitor Patrick

POLITICAL BETRAYAL

*"Is that what they told you?" asked Maureen Haughey about her husband's fall*

O'Connor, that Haughey, while alighting from his horse "Marshall", had reached up to catch a drainpipe to steady himself. The horse sprang forward, and the pipe broke under the strain of Haughey's weight and he fell to the ground.

Medical evidence stated that Haughey suffered a fractured skull, torn right eardrum, broken right collar bone and a fractured vertebra. He had severe concussion. Significantly, the doctor who oversaw his treatment in the Mater Hospital, Professor Senator Brian Alton, did not attend the press conference to corroborate the medical evidence. Alton, who prepared the medical report with the assistance of Dr Billy Hederman, was Haughey's personal physician.

After the conference, the then deputy editor and political correspondent of the *Evening Herald*, the late Des Mullan, rang Maureen Haughey for extra details. He asked how high from the horse was the drainpipe that Haughey had grabbed.

Maureen Haughey's brief response said it all: "Is that what they are saying? Is that what they told you?" She then hung up the 'phone.

Now, for the first time, I can reveal startling new evidence I obtained from a soldier who was on duty at Leinster House on the night before the budget. (An elite, hand-picked team of Army personnel guard Leinster House every night.)

Private Jim McMahon revealed to me that Haughey was at Leinster House more than an hour after the attack. He explained: "Accompanied by my NCO, I went to the Wicker Gate at Leinster House, where we found Mr Haughey waiting for us. I noticed Mr Haughey stooped over

*Were Charlie's injuries really the result of a fall from his horse?*

and he seemed to be in agony. Mr Haughey said to us: 'How are ye lads?' He had a hankie in his hands and seemed to be rubbing blood from his neck and his chin.

"I observed Mr Haughey for approximately five to six minutes. He looked like death warmed up. He was balancing himself beside a pillar. It was as if he had fallen down drunk or was in a row. His condition was consistent with someone who had been embroiled in a row and badly beaten up."

At 1.30am, Haughey was driven out of the complex in a black saloon car by a military policeman, who returned roughly two hours later in a taxi. The military policeman, Christy Guilfoyle, whom I later interviewed in his Dublin home, would not state where he drove Haughey that morning.

Private McMahon added: "The officer who was in charge at Government Buildings warned me later 'not to say anything to anybody' about what happened."

Just two days before the "fall", Jack Lynch was told details of Haughey's involvement in the plot to import arms illegally. On April 29, he visited Haughey in the Mater Hospital, where, incidentally, a special ward was always reserved for Fianna Fáil VIPs.

Though Haughey was seemingly unable to speak at the time, Lynch demanded his resignation. A week later, Haughey was fired.

In the days that followed, rumours continued to circulate that Haughey's riding accident was not a genuine one.

PR guru Eoin Patton, who worked with Haughey in several general elections and was regarded as a close friend, told me that Haughey spoke to him about the incident some years later. In an interview in the Berkeley Court Hotel, Patton revealed that Haughey's driver, Max Webster, was reading a paper in the ministerial car while Haughey was receiving a hiding upstairs in the Grasshopper Inn. If he had known that his Minister was being beaten up, he could have drawn his gun and shot the two men.

Some years later after the event, Haughey also told Patton that when he arrived at Leinster House, he examined his budget speech which had been left for him by his secretary. He was then escorted to the back of Leinster House where he met two soldiers, one of whom drove him out of the complex. (This story confirms the evidence of Private Jim McMahon and NCO Christy Guilfoyle).

According to Eoin Patton, Haughey revealed to him that the fall-from-a-horse story "was all staged – it never happened."

I attempted to interview Max Webster at his home in Castleknock. He refused to speak to me and closed the door in my face.

The Garda file on the Grasshopper Inn incident is no longer in the Department. It was removed several years ago.

How did Haughey repay O'Malley for saving his career and his reputation? In his first government in 1979, he appointed him to the prestigious Ministry of Industry and Commerce. However, six years later, Haughey arranged for the expulsion of O'Malley from Fianna Fáil for "conduct unbecoming". O'Malley's "crime"? He repeatedly spoke out against Haughey's autocratic leadership.

## A DUBLIN DALLIANCE

Haughey's affair of twenty-seven years with journalist Terry Keane began around 1976, but as important as that was to become, he still managed another casual love affair with a woman in a house in west Dublin. The lady concerned was the wife of an internationally acclaimed singer who was on tour when Haughey made a brief appearance.

After he knocked at the door and his lady friend answered, they immediately began embracing passionately. This continued until they reached the couch in the sitting room. She began to take some clothes off when she stopped suddenly, hearing the loud sound of a car pulling up in the front of the house.

"Oh, my God, he's back early," she shouted as Haughey made for the back door and subsequently cleared the back wall of the semi-detached home, as the singer warbled a couple of words from "Hear my Song." It was a narrow escape for the Don Juan of Irish politics.

While he was Taoiseach, he had another romantic string to his bow. On every trip to the US, a senior Bord Fáilte official had a secret mission – to discreetly find a young, attractive lady for the visiting Haughey.

## A LOUIS VUITTON HANDBAG

Max Webster, Haughey's loyal driver, drove Terry Keane to Dublin Airport to collect the then Taoiseach who was returning from a two-day meeting in Paris with his friend, French President François Mitterrand. On their way into the city, Haughey reached for a parcel on the floor. It was a Louis Vuitton handbag which had cost him more than €4,000. "Oh, it's beautiful", said Terry Keane as she began going through its various pockets.

As Webster drove by the Royal Canal, she realised none of the pockets had any cash. After asking Max to slow the car down, she

# POLITICAL BETRAYAL

*Terry Keane and her daughter Madeleine with Charlie Haughey.*

lowered the back window and dumped her new handbag in the Canal…to the consternation of a shocked Taoiseach who shouted, "Oh, my God, woman! What have you done?"

## ADVICE TO A GARDA

When she needed to, Terry Keane abused her power as the Taoiseach's mistress. On one occasion, she was involved in a minor incident with a garda while travelling in a car near St Stephen's Green in Dublin city centre.

The car was driven by the late Angela Phelan, an Irish Independent columnist, who was stopped by a garda and asked for her driving licence and insurance. As Angela was fumbling in her handbag, a polished voice in an English accent shouted from the back of the car, "Why don't you tell him to fuck off?"

The garda promptly took out his notebook. Peering into the back of the car, he saw a woman in a long black dress sprawled on the floor. Clearly inebriated, Terry added, "Tell him he is looking at the most powerful woman in the country."

The Garda put away his notebook. She then added, "Ask him would he like a transfer to the Road Traffic Division in Inishvickillane!"

Sheepishly, the garda replied, "That's in Kerry isn't it?"

She pressed home her advantage: "Yes, it is an island in South Kerry...and there are no fucking roads!"

*Donogh O'Malley*

## WHO WAS JANE'S FATHER?

Who was the father of Terry Keane's first child, Jane, who was born out of wedlock? The story is a bit confusing because Terry relayed two different versions about Jane's father.

Writing in *The Sunday Times*, she told the nation that a little-known actor, Jimmy Donnelly, was the father. They had a "fling" in the mid-sixties, she wrote, after a row with her regular boyfriend, Ronan Keane, who would later become Chief Justice.

*Daragh O'Malley*

Another version, however, emerged after Terry was re-united with her daughter, who had been adopted in England by a family called de Burgh. Terry escorted her around Dublin to meet most of her friends, and on one occasion they dropped into the Shelbourne Hotel along with the late P. J. Mara, Haughey's press secretary.

While they were there, film actor Daragh O'Malley dropped into the lobby. Daragh was the only son of Donogh O'Malley, a man who had left a deep mark on Irish politics as a Minister for Education.

"Who is that young handsome man?" asked Terry.

"That's Daragh O'Malley, Donogh's son," Mara explained.

"Bring him over here," Terry ordered.

Introducing Jane to Daragh, Terry said: "I would like to introduce you to your stepsister"!

Everybody was stunned!

P. J. Mara later relayed the story to some TDs, one of whom passed it on to me.

A few weeks later I ran into Daragh, whom I knew well from Limerick. I asked him if the Shelbourne story was true. He immediately answered: "Yes"

He added, "That was the first indication I had that my father had an affair."

Jane later married Dublin-born Carl Carpenter. They are the parents of Holly Carpenter, later to become Miss Ireland.

## THE NAKED LADY

One evening in the autumn of 1988, Charlie and Terry were deep in conversation in a screened-off area of his favourite Italian restaurant in South Dublin, which prided itself in providing discreet dining privacy to important customers.

A waiter approached to ask, "How do you like your prawns, Mr Haughey?"

Haughey responded, "Like my women…naked!" They all laughed.

The bell rang at the restaurant door. Two female guests were welcomed by the proprietor and were shown to a reserved table. One of them was in her early forties with thick, shoulder-length dark hair, dark eyebrows, and of a big build. She glanced across to the private area and recognised Charlie and Terry. She caught Charlie looking towards her and nodded in recognition, but he immediately turned away from her glance to give his full attention to Terry Keane.

The woman got up from her table and said to her friend (who was a journalist), "I'm going to powder my nose."

Moments later she walked out of the toilet and made straight for Haughey – wearing only her panties and black knee-high boots!

"Now, do you recognise me?" she asked as she stood defiantly at the couple's table.

With remarkable restraint, Haughey placed his glass on the snow-white tablecloth. Terry Keane picked up a napkin and covered half of her face in embarrassment. She then picked up her handbag, took out her dark glasses and put them on.

To a stunned silence from other guests, the tall, semi-naked woman turned and slinked back to the powder room. A few moments later, she walked back to her table, settled herself in her chair, placing the white linen napkin on her knee. She lifted her glass of red wine, leaned forward to her colleague and whispered, "I hope my main course is not cold."

The shattered proprietor kept bowing and apologising as Charlie and Terry stood up from their table, collecting their two wine bottles which they corked. As the proprietor walked backwards, continuing to bow and apologise, he told them: "Please accept my apologies. That should not have happened in my restaurant. The meal is complimentary; please do come back again."

## THE NIGHT THE CHANDELIERS SHOOK

Charlie and Terry met at least twice a week in Le Coq Hardi restaurant in Dublin. When they arrived, proprietor John Howard and his wife Catherine personally greeted them, and they would then make their way to the special dining room upstairs, a magnificent Georgian room, where only the staff would see them.

The staff were well used to all their gestures. When Terry wanted more wine, she tipped her glass to the waiter, while Charlie simply raised a hand. Most of the time they were discreet, but sometimes they were seen holding hands. On one occasion, Terry was desperately trying to close the sliding doors for a late-night canoodle and had to have help from a waiter.

And then there was that special night remembered by everybody present – the night their lovemaking was so intense that the chandeliers in the restaurant shook! The diners downstairs began to giggle and laugh and eventually applauded as the noise of the lovemaking intensified.

The restaurant staff estimated that the weekly bill was never less than €1,000. No money was ever paid by Charlie at the restaurant; the bill was sent to him at government buildings and paid monthly.

I was able to establish that Haughey paid the bills from his own personal leader's account. I wrote firstly to the Office of the Comptroller and Auditor General, then John Purcell, and asked if he was aware if bills for the period August 1, 1988 to December 31, 1996 were paid personally by Haughey or did they come from public funds.

In reply to my query, Fergus O'Brien, private secretary to the Comptroller wrote: "This Office audits the expenditure charged to the Annual Accounts on a test basis and any serious breach of regularity propriety would be brought to the attention of the Comptroller and Auditor General. If he deems it appropriate to do so, he may include a reference to the issue in his report to Dáil Éireann. I can confirm that there was no such reference to the former Taoiseach's expenses in the period mentioned in your letter. It may well be that the Department of the Taoiseach can provide the information sought by you and I would suggest that you might contact that Department in this regard."

We did. The reply from Ann Whelan, head of the finance unit at the Department of the Taoiseach read: "I wish to advise you that in the period 1987 to February 1992, the records of the Department show one payment to Le Coq Hardi Restaurant – for a lunch hosted by the former Taoiseach on December 4, 1991, for the then British Prime Minister (Margaret Thatcher) in Government Buildings."

Apparently, there was no serious breach of "regularity propriety" by Haughey. However, the Moriarty Tribunal, which later examined his finances in detail, disclosed that he spent €26,470 per month on wining and dining Terry Keane and buying many presents and holidays for her.

When Terry dined in the Coq Hardi, she sometimes ordered a case of vintage wine. It is not known who paid for it. Several times Terry brought in her own friends. On one memorable occasion, On one memorable occasion, she invited a close friend to dine with her. The lunch came to €45 and the drink to €450! The bill was invoiced to Haughey.

Haughey liked to be served by a French-speaking waiter, as he was fluent in French. His usual tip for lunch was €10 and for dinner €20.

Terry had expensive tastes. She loved lobster, while Charlie preferred oysters the French way – a little vinegar, baby onions and lemon. He was also partial to asparagus. For the main course, he would generally choose fish – either monkfish or sole. He never ate desert. Terry frequently did.

She would start lunch with Dom Perignon (at least €100 a bottle) and a packet of Marlboro cigarettes. Charlie, who fancied himself as a connoisseur of vintage wine, would begin with Puligny Montrachet White 80. And for dinner he generally chose Calon-Ségur Bordeaux.

After the wine he drank claret. While he arrived early to avoid the crowd, he left promptly after midnight. Terry would generally stay until 4 or 5 a.m., drinking Muscat de Beaumes-de-Venise.

Charlie's guests included people like Nobel Peace winner Seamus Heaney and the glamorous travel entrepreneur Gillian Bowler. Terry sometimes brought an entourage that included family and friends.

## A SPECIAL NIGHT

Staff remember another special night in Le Coq Hardi – the evening in September 1994 when Charlie was celebrating his 69th birthday.

POLITICAL BETRAYAL

*Le Coq Hardi, where Terry and Charlie dined in a private room upstairs.*

Terry's present was thought-provoking and audacious – a painting of a mermaid lying on a bed. He was in no doubt that the mermaid was Terry in a sexy rear-view pose. The lady had style.

Their regular get-togethers were not confined to the Coq Hardi. They also had the use of a tastefully furnished mews in Wellington Road in Ballsbridge, the owner of which had received a favour from Charlie when he was Minister for Finance. They also used a place near the Berkeley Court Hotel and a restaurant called Armstrong's Barn in Annamoe, Co. Wicklow, where the neighbours were film director John Boorman and triple Oscar winner Daniel Day-Lewis. They made use of the place in the middle of the week. They insisted on fresh flowers before they arrived in separate cars. Charlie left his driver in the scenic village of Roundwood, less than five miles away.

The Berkeley Court in Ballsbridge was another favourite haunt. Thanks to his excellent relationship with the owner, the late P. V. Doyle, Charlie had the use of a suite which he and Terry frequented at least once a week. The bill for the fare they enjoyed there was between €300 and €600 per week and sometimes as high as €1,000. The former Taoiseach operated a similar arrangement to Le Coq Hardi. The bill was never sent to his home in Kinsealy but posted to his office at Government buildings. No bill was ever sent without being vetted by the proprietor himself. According to Ann

*The source of his silk shirts: Charvet's in Paris.*

Whelan, head of finance unit at the Department of the Taoiseach, no payment by the department was made to the Berkeley Court on behalf of Haughey.

As with Le Coq Hardi, Terry Keane brought her own entourage to the Berkeley Court. She regularly ordered cases of wine. Most of the time she signed Haughey's name to it. After he retired, she was seldom seen in the hotel.

## TRIPS ABROAD

There were numerous trips together out of Ireland. On many occasions, they visited France – Charlie's favourite country. But it was unusual for the Taoiseach to have non-Government personnel aboard the Government jet. This came about after a row between Haughey and his Minister for Finance, Albert Reynolds. The Department of Finance had overseen the Government jet. Any non-Government personnel had to be cleared by them. Albert Reynolds brought a party of financial journalists on the jet to Milan during Ireland's EC Presidency and when Haughey heard about it, he almost blew a fuse. He told Reynolds that the jet was for him and could only be used by other ministers in "special circumstances". Charlie kicked up such a fuss that Reynolds told him to take total charge of the jet. In future, the Taoiseach's office would clear all non-Government personnel.

While it was a headache for Charlie to have to oversee its use, it meant that he could bring anybody he wanted on board without any questions being asked. Friends recall Terry ringing home on one occasion from the exclusive George V Hotel in Paris. Terry, who had travelled on the Government jet, told them she was using a circular bed and had difficulty finding her head! While she was on the 'phone, Charlie was in the shower.

He bought silk dressing gowns from Charvet. Terry admired them so much that he brought six of them back to her after his next visit to Paris. During that visit, his then Foreign Minister, Brian Lenihan accompanied him. The other members of his entourage included his private secretary, Pádraig Ó hAnracháin, and Government Press Secretary, Frank Dunlop. After their brief visit to President d'Estaing, they were free for the rest of the afternoon. Charlie announced to his colleagues: "We're going shopping!".

At the entrance to Charvet's, they were met by the patron and escorted to a plush waiting area while Charlie went in. A couple of moments later, Charlie came out with parcels. When Frank Dunlop looked closely at him, he said: "They are my shirts, Frank." He then pointed to them and gesticulated to the patron, explaining: "They are my security." In honour of the occasion, Charlie's "security" men were presented with a silk tie each. Terry was also given Louis Vuitton luggage – six matching suitcases worth €3,000, which she used for several years.

When Charlie had money, he was generous. But when he was out of office, he had to be more careful about his spending. On one occasion, after Terry moved to fashionable Ranelagh in south Dublin, she told Charlie: "I have to have an alarm system." Charlie had an elaborate system installed for €3,500. On another occasion, her car did not start. She called Charlie: "I need a car and I need it now!" At the time, he was out of office; all he could afford was a second-hand Renault 5.

## TERRY IN HOSPITAL

Terry was involved in a freak accident when a lighted match singed her eyebrows, and she was taken to St Vincent's Hospital. The only bed available was in a public ward, which did not please her. She phoned Charlie who told her to try to move to the Mater Hospital on the north side of Dublin, because he had "no pull" in St Vincent's.

When fellow patients attempted to talk to her, she pulled her curtain across saying, "We have nothing in common." She complained so much about the "dreadful people" she was with that Haughey arranged for lunch to be sent from the fashionable Patrick Gilbaud restaurant. She eventually got a private ward. One of her first visitors was businessman Gerry Jones, a tall man with a black patch over his eye and a close friend of Charlie. He offered his chair when Charlie arrived, but Charlie refused. But Charlie, always conscious of his small stature, could not contain himself: "I know you are taller than I am. There is no need to rub it in."

While in hospital, Terry complained about the television set, which was coin operated. She told Charlie she wanted one of her own...a white one. A cream one arrived, and she kicked up another storm. She fired a tray at the set saying, "I said I wanted a white one." That television went back to her house. When her husband, Ronan Keane, asked her where she got it, she told him that her friend, Noelle Campbell-Sharpe, "got a present of it and gave it to me."

During a holiday in the Canaries, Terry was involved in another freak accident. Part of a stainless-steel covering had come loose, and she tripped on it and sustained a nasty cut in her leg. She was rushed to a clinic in Puerto Rico where it was crudely sewn up with black gut. Later, on the phone to Charlie, she sobbed, "My ankles are my crowning glory and they are ruined!" Charlie got on to the head of Aer Rianta, Martin Dully, and asked him to arrange a wheelchair at Dublin Airport for her return. Meanwhile, Terry was busy in the Canaries, loading a canvas bag with bottles of liquor. When the jet arrived at Dublin Airport, she was first to disembark. Husband Ronan was there to greet her and wheeled her off. He escorted her through customs, a rug cleverly concealing the bag of duty-free booze!

A Terry Keane put-down could be devastating. During the wilderness years after Jack Lynch had sacked him, close friend P. J. Mara drove Charlie around the country. A rendezvous with Terry had been arranged and Mara joined them for a few minutes. In a frosty voice, Terry snapped to Haughey, "Tell your driver to wait in the car!" She also had a minor brush with Charlie's son Ciaran who was at the time seeing a Danish beauty. Terry reprimanded Charlie: "Keep your son and his Danish hairdresser out of my social circle".

Terry spent a lot of time with her neighbours, the late Professor Gus Martin and his wife, Claire. On one occasion late at night, she rang Charlie. "Your response to Margaret Thatcher in the Dáil to-day was superb," she said. Then turning to Gus Martin and covering the mouthpiece, she whispered: "What did Charlie actually say?"

Then there was the night Charlie accompanied Gus Martin and Claire to the Abbey Theatre to see a production of John B. Keane's The Field. Gus was Chairman of the National Theatre and had been pleading for years with Charlie, a keen supporter of the arts, to see an Abbey play.

After the first act, Gus remarked that Haughey would empathise with the main character, Bull McCabe, played by the late Ray McAnally, after the interval.

"You will see the greed, nastiness and avarice of this bully in the second period," he promised.

"What do you mean?" said Charlie. "I'm with this character right

*Terry with her friend Noelle Campbell-Sharpe.*

from the opening act."

## TERRY'S BETRAYAL OF CHARLIE

At what turned out to be her final lunch with Charlie in Le Coq Hardi, Terry revealed to Charlie that she was going to disclose their affair on the "Late Late Show" the following night, and that she had completed a book deal with *The Sunday Times*.

Clearly stunned, Haughey asked her to reconsider. He offered to match the Sunday Times offer for her story if she pulled out of the "Late Late Show" appearance.

Coldly, Terry looked at her former lover and told him it was her story, and she was going to reveal it. Charlie immediately stood up from his chair, walked out of the restaurant, and never saw his lover of twenty-seven years again.

It has been estimated that her betrayal of Haughey earned her nearly €300,000. According to a statement on May 21, 1999, she was paid a total of €65,000 for four installments "in respect of the serialisation of my book by *The Sunday Times*". She was also paid €50,000 per annum for a period of two years as a weekly columnist with the paper. She also received an estimated €40,000 for two articles in the *Irish Daily Mail* and the *Irish Star*.

In that statement of May, 1999, Terry explained why she appeared on the "Late Late Show" and wrote the articles in *The Sunday Times*:

"Once I became aware that Mr Kevin O'Connor was about to make public the fact of my relationship with Mr Haughey in what Mr O'Connor himself describes as a 'racy account of the life of Charles Haughey and his mistress, Terry Keane' I felt I had no choice other than to allow the true version of my relationship with Mr Haughey into the public domain. For this reason, I was grateful to accept the invitation to appear on the Late Late Show."

The big question asked by many is how much, if anything, did Maureen Haughey know about the affair between her husband and Terry Keane. It is known that she did receive an anonymous letter in the late 1980s and was worried enough about the contents to consult the late Pádraig Ó hAnnracháin, close friend and advisor to her husband. He advised her to disregard the letter: "Never take any notice of anonymous letters".

Some days later, she was alone in her kitchen, avidly reading the "Keane Edge" column in the *Sunday Independent*. Her daughter-in-law passing by, heard her sobbing and saw tears in her eyes.

# HAUGHEY AND NORTHERN IRELAND

## HEROES OF THE ARMS CRISIS

In May 1970, what came to be known as the Arms Crisis exploded on the nation after the Taoiseach, Jack Lynch, sacked two of his most prominent Ministers: Haughey, who was Minister for Finance, and Neil Blaney, Minister for Agriculture. It was alleged that both men had been involved in illegal attempts to import guns into the country for us in the North, which was then in turmoil.

There were two heroes of the crisis, both of whom succeeded in eliciting the truth about both ministers. They were the long-serving Secretary to the Department of Justice, Peter Berry, and, to a lesser extent, the Fine Gael Leader, Liam Cosgrave, who played a significant role in forcing Lynch to act.

Lynch said he was informed of the arms crisis on April 20, 1970, by Berry, who had been secretary to thirteen previous Ministers for Justice – almost an Irish version of J. Edgar Hoover!

Almost at the same time, Liam Cosgrave was being briefed in detail about the arms plot by a highly placed Special Branch member. Cosgrave had earlier tipped off his friend Ned Murphy, the *Sunday Independent* political correspondent, whose excellent exclusive was spiked by the then editor, Hector Legge. He told Ned, one of the most respected journalists of his era, that the story was so dramatic it should only be raised in the Dáil.

Peter Berry decided to act after receiving a damning phone call from Charles Haughey.

That call, later revealed in Berry's diaries in *Magill* magazine, was made on Saturday, April 18, 1970, when Haughey asked him if he was aware of a "certain cargo" that was due at Dublin Airport the next day. Berry replied: "Yes, Minister." Haughey then came to the crunch. He asked if the cargo would be allowed through Customs if a guarantee were given that it would go directly to the North. Knowing that such an importation was illegal and fully aware of Government policy, Berry replied: "No."

Haughey's response said a lot: "I think that is a bad decision." He then asked if "the man from Mayo" (the then Minister for Justice, Mícheál Ó Móráin) knew about this? He was told that Ó Móráin was aware of the arms plot.

Haughey asked another crucial question: "What will happen when it arrives." Berry's reply was succinct: "It will be grabbed."

There is no doubt that Haughey's response implicated him in the whole arms plot: "I had better have it called off." He was told by Berry that there was no possibility of the arms consignment getting through "because there was a ring of steel around the airport" which had been placed at his discretion.

Haughey's later defence in court was that he knew nothing about the arms importation. But the Berry phone call was crucial in confirming his full implication in the arms plot. Berry gave testimony to this effect at the two arms trials later in September and October.

In the meantime, Berry felt frustrated with Mícheál Ó Móráin, who at that crucial time was still practising as a solicitor and was not available in his Ministerial office when urgently needed. Berry decided to contact President Eamon de Valera by calling on him in the Áras. Berry told him that information of a serious nature had come into his possession, involving the security of the nation. Berry had a simple question: was he justified in bringing it to the attention of the Taoiseach, Jack Lynch?

Typically, Dev did not request details. He just asked if Berry was certain of the facts. Berry assured him the facts were correct. The President made it clear he had a duty not only to the Minister but to the Government as a whole. He advised him to speak to Lynch.

Having left the Áras, Berry rang the President thirty minutes later: "A Uachtarán, is it okay if I mention to the Taoiseach that you advised me to speak to him?" Dev paused for a few moments: "No, I would prefer if you keep me out it."

On April 29, Lynch asked for Haughey's resignation for his

# HAUGHEY AND NORTHERN IRELAND

*Two heroes of the Arms Crisis: Liam Cosgrave (above) and Peter Berry.*

alleged involvement in the arms plot. Lynch said later that Haughey appeared unable to speak at that time. Subsequently Haughey asked for time to consider his position.

In the meantime, Liam Cosgrave heard about the plot from a senior Special Branch source and became aware that Lynch was dithering and procrastinating about taking a firm decision. Cosgrave sought an urgent private meeting with Lynch and bluntly told him that, unless he acted promptly, he would expose him in the Dáil.

In a dramatic statement from the Government Information Service early on May 6, Jack Lynch announced that he had fired two of his Ministers, Charles Haughey and Neil Blaney, for their alleged involvement in the arms plot. Knowing that Cosgrave was on his case, Lynch had no other option.

A marathon debate in the Dáil began on Friday, May 8, and continued for thirty-seven and a half hours until late on Saturday night, May 9. The debate gave the Taoiseach an opportunity to make his first public explanation of the sacking and to present his case against the two ministers.

Blaney spoke in the debate, and Haughey issued a statement from his home. But neither could offer a defence, partly because they were still members of Fianna Fáil and had to strictly keep to the party line.

Charles Haughey issued his denial in a statement from his solicitors. He said: "I regret that on medical advice I cannot make a personal statement in Dáil Éireann concerning the termination of my office as a member of the Government. Since becoming a Minister I have endeavoured to the best of my ability to serve my country, Dáil Éireann, and the Government. I have never at any time acted in breach of the trust reposed in me, and I regret that I am now compelled to refer to the circumstances that brought an end to my membership of the Government.

"The Taoiseach informed the Dáil that he requested my resignation on the grounds that he was convinced that not even the slightest suspicion should attach to any member of the Government. I fully subscribe to that view. So far as I have been able to gather, the Taoiseach received information of a nature, which, in his opinion, cast some suspicions on me. I have not had the opportunity to examine or test such information or the quality of its source or sources.

"In the meantime, however, I now categorically state that at no time have I taken part in any illegal importation or attempted importation of arms into this country."

The clear inference in Haughey's statement was that any attempted importation of arms was made with the authority of the Minister for Defence, Jim Gibbons, and therefore legal.

His colleague Neil Blaney spoke with characteristic bluntness. "I

*Partners: Charles Haughey and Neil Blaney at the time of the Arms Crisis.*

want to say I have run no guns; I have procured no guns; I have paid for no guns and I have not provided any money to pay for guns. Anyone who says otherwise is not telling the truth." He attacked those spreading innuendos and trying to link his name to illegal organisations and "that lousy outfit Saor Éire." He defended his own and Haughey's brothers who had been accused by Liam Cosgrave (under privilege of parliament) of gun running.

He went into his family background and told how he was born while his father was a Free State prisoner under sentence of death, how he had been pulled out of his cot as an infant by Special Branch detectives searching his family home for arms. As a boy, he had fought what he termed "Blueshirt bullies."

Cosgrave claimed that but for his action in going to the Taoiseach, the whole affair would have been concealed from the public. The people, he asserted, had "been betrayed with their own money." He said that Ireland could thank God for the second time in fifty years that they had the Fine Gael party to maintain and assert the people's rights. He declared that he and his party had prevented a civil war of a religious character.

Jack Lynch gave his explanation of how information had come to him from the Special Branch and the Department of Justice (Peter Berry) and how he had conducted his own investigation. The two ministers concerned had denied involvement in the plot as alleged, but he could not allow the finger of suspicion to point at any member of the Government.

He paid tribute to the men he had dismissed. They were "able and brilliant", and it was "a sad day that our ministerial paths had to part." They had strong family traditions of service to the country "in the fight for freedom", which his family had not. But Jack Lynch insisted that as Taoiseach his "primary duty was to the country" and he "did not shirk it."

He ended by accusing the Opposition of irresponsibility in trying to convince the country that a national emergency was on hand, with bogus threats of a coup d'état or a civil war. They were "playing with lives" because of the tense situation in the North, and they had demonstrated clearly that they could offer no responsible alternative to a Fianna Fáil Government.

Winding up the debate for the opposition, Dr Garret FitzGerald (later to become Taoiseach) told the country what was behind the dismissals. He said that both Blaney and Haughey were acting in close association with the IRA; the Justice Minister Mícheál Ó Móráin had actively assisted them in importing arms; Defence Minister Jim Gibbons had been an agent provocateur who had betrayed all three to the Taoiseach; Captain James Kelly, described as the "fall guy", had been used by Gibbons to bring about the downfall of the three ministers.

He described Blaney as a second Paisley – ruthless, sinister and ambitious. Haughey was a man of great ability, but arrogant and unscrupulous, while Kevin Boland (who resigned as Minister for Local Government in sympathy with the ministers) was sincere, but misguided and irresponsible.

*Des O'Malley: a controversial meeting with Haughey.*

When the Dáil debate concluded, Haughey was forced to swallow his pride and vote confidence in the Taoiseach who had sacked him, and Jack Lynch got approval for his new Ministers by 73 votes to 66.

Charges were brought in late May 1970 against Haughey, Blaney, Captain James Kelly and two other men, John Kelly a republican from Belfast, and Albert Luykx, a Howth businessman who was a native of Belgium. They were accused of a conspiracy to import arms.

Interestingly, when the Special Branch arrived at Kinsealy to serve the charges on Haughey, there was a member of the judiciary in his drawing room. No explanation was ever given for this. Could he have been a relic of the past – like the secret courts in the sixties that Haughey was running with the co-operation of the judiciary? He could also have been offering legal advice to Haughey.

Subsequently, charges against Neil Blaney were refused in the District Court and, following accusations of bias against the judge, Justice Aindrias Ó Caoimh (a son-in-law of President de Valera) the first trial in the Central Criminal Court collapsed on September 29, 1970. A second trial of the four remaining defendants lasted from

October 6 to October 23. All the defendants were found not guilty. A crowd of some 500 people outside the courthouse went wild as the verdict reached them.

At the second trial, Mr Justice Henchy bluntly spelled out the truth of what had transpired during evidence. Somebody was lying, he said. "Either Charles Haughey or Jim Gibbons was a liar and either Charles Haughey or Peter Berry was a liar." Within fifty minutes, the jury returned with a verdict of not guilty against all the accused.

Charles Haughey believed at the time (and many shared his view) that British intelligence could have been responsible for leaking the arms crisis story.

Back in August 1970, Haughey met the new Minister for Justice, 31-year-old Des O'Malley, who was appointed in May after the Taoiseach asked for Ó Móráin's resignation. A nephew of the late Minister for Education, Donogh O'Malley, he was known in Leinster House as "the man from uncle."

In his memoirs, *Conduct Unbecoming*, O'Malley explained how this controversial meeting with Haughey came about before the trial took place. Haughey had approached him at the Tralee races and told him he had a problem of a "personal family nature" and would appreciate a meeting. O'Malley agreed to meet him the following week in Leinster House. When he mentioned it to Peter Berry his secretary, he thought it was "not a good idea."

At the meeting, Haughey began to talk about a close relative who was in some kind of trouble.

According to O'Malley, "It quickly became obvious that it was just a ruse for a meeting about the arms trial."

Haughey came to the nitty-gritty. "Will Peter Berry give evidence?"

It was obvious why Haughey wanted to know this, considering the damning phone call he had already made to Peter Berry at his Dartry home in Dublin some months previously.

O'Malley's response was: "Of course."

Haughey then showed his true form. "Is there anything that can be done?"

O'Malley then realised that Haughey was attempting to interfere with material evidence. O'Malley reminded Haughey that material in the book of evidence, including statements made by Berry, "could not and would not be altered."

Realising he was not getting anywhere, Haughey then began to berate Berry and O'Malley decided to end the meeting.

Later, O'Malley revealed the contents of the meeting to Berry and was surprised with Berry's response. Berry told O'Malley that the purpose of telling him what happened was to prevail on him to do what Haughey wanted. He accepted that he should never have had the meeting with Haughey who was clearly attempting to meddle with the judicial system.

One could also ask why O'Malley did not communicate with the Garda authorities subsequently and disclose how Haughey had attempted to interfere with material evidence.

During the Dáil debate, Brian Lenihan, who was then Minister for Transport, asked permission from Fianna Fáil whip Michael Carty for a "pair" with the opposition. That in effect meant that the opposition would withdraw one of their members if there was a vote. Brian Lenihan told Carty that he wanted to visit Haughey, who was still recovering from the Grasshopper Inn beating. Carty agreed to the request.

Listening to the conversation in the room was the late Erskine Childers, who would later become an outstanding President. Childers, who was Tánaiste in the Lynch government, waited until Lenihan left the room and then told Carty that as far as he was concerned, Haughey was a traitor and it was "disgraceful" that a member of the Cabinet should be visiting a person who was "guilty of treason." In any other country, said Childers, Haughey would have been tried for treason.

*Kevin Boland: "Haughey was not telling the truth."*

## BOLAND ON THE ARMS CRISIS

Kevin Boland spoke about the crisis in 1998 during a special interview on the popular Vincent Browne radio programme. He told Browne that he was aware of the arms importation before the crisis erupted. Charlie Haughey came to his office to tell him about the shipment of arms that was going to be acquired.

Vincent Browne: "I must put to you, Kevin, that Charles Haughey said under oath during the course of the arms trial that he knew nothing about it. You are saying now that he not only knew about it at the time, but he told you about it in advance?"

Boland: "That's right. Yes."

Browne: "What did you say to him when he told you this?"

Boland: "I said I hope you have a reliable chain of authority who will ensure that these weapons will only be used when there is no alternative to going in and helping the Civil Rights people who were being beaten up in the Six Counties at the time."

Browne: "What did you feel about him saying...subsequently when he denied in the course of the arms crisis, when he denied it under oath in the High Court that he knew anything about this? You knew this to be untrue. You also knew that his denial jeopardised the defence offered by his co-accused – namely John Kelly, Captain James Kelly, and Albert Luykx. Did you not feel some obligation to go and say 'Look it, this isn't true?'

Boland: "Well, I didn't do it anyway."

Browne: "Kevin, the Fianna Fáil party was divided down the middle between the factions believing Jim Gibbons and the factions believing Charles Haughey. You were perceived as being one of Haughey's allies and you are saying that Gibbons was essentially telling the truth as he knew it and Haughey was not doing so."

Boland: "Well he (Haughey) was telling a certain amount of the truth, but when he denied that he was involved in it, then he was not telling the truth."

Later, Boland revealed that he tried to get Charles Haughey to join his new party, Aontacht Éireann. Haughey, however, said he was staying where he was because "that's the place to be if you want to stick a knife in a man's back. You want to be close to him."

Browne: "Who was he referring to?"

Boland: "He was thinking of (Jack) Lynch of course."

## THE ARMY'S SECRET POLICY

We can reveal that the Army Intelligence section had a secret policy that included recruiting prominent journalists, TDs, and prominent gardaí.

During the northern troubles, the section regularly contacted political journalist Ned Murphy to verify certain information. Ned Murphy, who died in the 1980s, was one of the most influential journalists of his era, breaking many exclusives during his time as political correspondent of the *Sunday Independent*.

We also understand that well placed gardaí – particularly in the Special Branch – were regularly used and were paid handsomely for their information. Some of the money was lodged in accounts in the Isle of Man.

Army Intelligence also attempted to recruit influential TDs – mainly Fianna Fáil and Fine Gael. One Fianna Fáil TD who came from an influential family and did not wish to be named told me about his encounter with an Army recruiting officer. "The officer asked for a meeting in a Dublin Hotel. I was flabbergasted when he requested me to work for Army Intelligence.

"He told me that he would require regular briefings of what was happening at the secret parliamentary party meetings. He revealed that it would be lucrative for me. I would be secretly given the rank of captain and on retirement would receive the pension of a captain." The TD, who has since lost his seat, rejected the offer.

## HAUGHEY'S PEACE MOVES

According to new evidence from sources within the Special Branch, Charles Haughey had substantial contacts with high ranking members of the IRA while he was Minister for Finance and during the wilderness years when he was out of Government. He had meetings with Cathal Goulding, head of the IRA, to discuss how weapons could be moved throughout the North. When questioned later by the Government to explain his meetings, Haughey lied that he had been asked to meet an individual whom he did not know and that it had not been an important encounter.

After his sacking by Jack Lynch for his alleged involvement in arms smuggling, he was in touch with Belfast republican John Kelly and IRA leader Joe Cahill. He promised in a Special Branch memorandum to pass on "anything he hears", but insisted that his name be kept out of it.

When he was Taoiseach in 1987, he was aware of soundings by the republican leadership about finding a way to end the IRA campaign. But, despite all his contacts, he never grasped the opportunity to begin a "peace process" in the way Albert Reynolds later did. This seems to contrast with the boldness of many of his

*Martin Mansergh, Haughey's adviser on the North.*

decisions.

Indeed, Haughey briefed Reynolds about the various peace moves before leaving office, telling him that if he wanted to make something of it, he might like to keep his Northern adviser, Dr Martin Mansergh on the team. (Mansergh was so important to the peace process that even John Bruton tried to keep him on board, but Martin stayed loyal to Fianna Fáil). It was apparently about the only thing an embittered Haughey briefed the new Taoiseach on (he had blamed Reynolds for his downfall).

Reynolds not only kept the clever and immensely experienced Mansergh on board but decided to make the ending of Northern violence a central policy of his administration. The Labour Party claims that the briefing Dick Spring received on the prospects for peace was a key factor in its controversial decision to join forces with Fianna Fáil to form a government.

Insiders claim that things went a lot further under Haughey's government than has been generally acknowledged. The final draft of the Downing Street Declaration – the key document in the process towards the IRA ceasefire – was drafted by Mansergh during Haughey's final year in power in 1991.

Given his substantial contacts with the IRA and his vast experience in Government, it could be argued that Haughey could have been the man to broker the ceasefire. However, he did not know he was going to be ejected from office by the John O'Connell ultimatum in 1992. Also, he had good reason to be cautious. The events of the arms trial must have made him acutely sensitive to the dangers of getting involved in Northern affairs. Those same events made him a figure of huge suspicion to almost everyone outside of Fianna Fáil. Certainly, they gave him some standing with republicans. But he was not to be trusted.

History has yet to deliver its final verdict on whether Haughey was right to move slowly on the peace process, and whether Reynolds's all-action approach forced the various parties into negotiations before they were ready. Haughey judged that Sinn Féin was not ready when the first approaches came. His private secretary and friend Padraig Ó hAnnracháin had confidential discussions with Gerry Adams, but the impetus came to nothing after the Enniskillen bombing, which one insider describes as a "traumatic shock" not just to the Haughey government but also to many people in the republican movement. That bombing in 1987 killed eleven and injured sixty-four people, one dying thirteen years after being in a coma.

The Redemptorist priest Fr Alex Reid, an unsung hero during the peace negotiations, played a key role in the entire peace process. He arranged two meetings between Ó hAnnracháin, Gerry Adams, and other senior Sinn Féin people in the Redemptorist monastery in Dundalk. The contacts were made in great secrecy, and even that inspired peace maker and noble peace prize winner, the late John Hume, was unaware that these meetings were taking place. But the government representatives found that Sinn Féin seemed unaware of what would be required of them and especially of the IRA if they were to enter the political process. Ó hAnnracháin gave this assessment to Haughey, and contacts were broken off.

It was not until 1991 that the situation seemed to have changed sufficiently for another attempt. Fr Reid again was the go-between for the Hume-Adams dialogue which began in the late 1980s and lasted ten years. John Hume met Haughey and briefed him on the results of his meetings. Martin Mansergh was called in to put some of this down on paper. The result was a first draft of what became the Downing Street Declaration.

It was widely assumed at the time that Hume had given the government a document setting out their ideas for a peace process. But sources in the then government insist that Haughey, through Mansergh, was centrally involved in the drafting and that it contained the essence of the Downing Street Declaration. So far, the British had not been involved. During the EU summit in 1991, Haughey briefly mentioned what was going on to Prime Minister John Major. Though non-committal, he showed some interest. However, it transpired later that the British were having their own contacts with the IRA, without the Irish Government knowing anything about it.

Sinn Féin and John Hume put pressure on Haughey to arrange a meeting with the then Sinn Féin leader, Gerry Adams. But, like Reynolds after him, he insisted there could be no such meeting until the IRA had called off its campaign. Haughey believed that, particularly with his record, the issue was so sensitive he might have to resign as Taoiseach if the story of the contacts broke. So, from his own point of view, he was taking a considerable risk for peace. Haughey was conscious that no democratic government could broker a peace deal, while violence continued. He was more vulnerable than Reynolds who carried no Northern baggage – so he moved very cautiously.

Sources close to Haughey think he regretted this caution with Sinn Féin later, seeing what Albert Reynolds achieved. Gerry Adams, after his secret talks with John Hume, thought it was possible to break Sinn Féin's isolation, even if the IRA campaign continued. He proposed a "pan-nationalist" front of political parties north and south to push for a political settlement, but did not include an IRA ceasefire in the plan. He believed there would be grassroots support within Fianna Fáil for such a plan. But Haughey's representatives were instructed to tell Adams that no Irish government could even appear to be involved in any alliance while the violence continued.

Haughey supporters, however, believe that Reynolds could not have brokered the IRA ceasefire without the earlier work done under Haughey's government.

## BOMB SCARE

In 1981, the Fianna Fáil Government managed to keep under wraps a serious bomb scare in a hotel in Letterkenny.

At that time, Haughey as Taoiseach was chairing a Fianna Fáil meeting in the hotel when the members were alerted to the bomb scare and had to clear the premises. It turned out that the bomb was in a cistern in the toilet.

The bomb squad were alerted in Dublin and later arrived in a helicopter. The bomb squad operator looked at the bomb and saw there was no timer – in other words it could go off at any moment. He asked his colleague to provide him with a bag. A few moments later he coolly walked out of the hotel with the bomb in the bag and boarded the nearby helicopter. They immediately flew towards the army headquarters in Donegal and dismantled the bomb.

In subsequent investigations, the Gardaí discovered that the UVF were responsible for placing the bomb. It wasn't the only time the UVF attempted to take out Haughey. There is a letter on file on UVF notepaper in Government buildings, stating that they had plans to assassinate the Taoiseach.

## WAS HAUGHEY AN IRA SPY ?

Was former Taoiseach, Charles Haughey acting as an informer for the IRA during a brief period of his long career?

That is the only conclusion to be drawn from new evidence I have obtained from his time as Minister for Finance and later in the wilderness years after he was sacked by Jack Lynch.

After the British army marched through Derry on August 15, 1969, as the troubles escalated, Haughey had a secret meeting with Cathal Goulding, then IRA chief of staff. According to a reliable source within the Special Branch, they discussed how weapons could be moved in the north.

Haughey, apparently pleaded with Goulding to stop the destruction of foreign-owned property in the South. In return, the IRA would be assisted in moving weapons. This would suggest that a source within the Gardaí would contact the RUC, who would turn a blind eye to illegal weapons freely moving throughout the North.

When requested later by members of the Government to explain his controversial meeting with Goulding, Haughey lied that he had been asked to meet an individual whom he didn't know and that it had not been an important encounter.

It has also been established that in October 1969 he secretly met the then British Ambassador to Ireland, Sir Andrew Gilchrist. The topic discussed was the possible British terms for a united Ireland. In view of the new revelations, it can now be asked... did he convey those discussions with Sir Andrew to the IRA?

It is now known that while he was Minister for Finance in the late 1960s he was tapping the phone of his boss, Jack Lynch!

As the Arms Crisis exploded on the nation in May 1970, Lynch assured every member of the Dáil that their phones had not been tapped by the Government. It turned out that his assurance was not correct. According to a highly placed Special Branch source, Lynch did not know about the most audacious and sensational 'phone tap that was being orchestrated at that time.

Opposite Government buildings, a technician was on duty on a Saturday morning in the Merrion Street telephone exchange. He spotted something unusual. The attentive official, Brian Killeen, found a parallel tap on the main distribution frame. Astonished, he

POLITICAL BETRAYAL

*Haughey loads his shotgun before starting the Dingle Regatta in 1994.*

PHOTOGRAPH: DON MACMONAGLE

brought the discovery to the attention of his superior, Jim Dermody. The two men double-checked that it was a genuine tap – and then they made another sensational discovery: the tap was on the phone of the Taoiseach. And worse: it was directly linked to Haughey's office.

A thorough investigation was carried out by senior members of the Special Branch to find out who was responsible. Apparently, Haughey was questioned but denied all knowledge. Nobody was ever charged, and the whole incident was eventually let drop.

Knowing now that Haughey had many contacts over the years with the IRA, it can justifiably be asked if he relayed the contents of Lynch's conversations to senior members of the organisation.

The Special Branch, who were monitoring Haughey for many years and regularly tapping his phone, disclosed later to the Government that he had several meetings with leading members of the IRA, some at his mansion in Kinsealy. But one of the most sensational of all was when Haughey was out of power. It has now been established that the Jack Lynch Government received a memorandum on his IRA activities in 1973. The covert, top-secret memo from the Special Branch, which I have seen, read:

"Mr Charles Haughey is still in touch with the Provisional IRA through John Kelly and Joe Cahill. He told them he was not in a position to do anything for them at present but that he hoped to be back in the Government in a few months' time and would press for a stronger line on the North. He told them that Special Branch, Dublin Castle, were still receiving information from inside the republican movement but not as much as heretofore. He promises to pass on anything he hears on that aspect but to keep his name out of it."

That was an extraordinary memorandum from many points of view. It demonstrated that Haughey was prepared to act virtually as a spy for the IRA. By stating that he was "not in a position to do anything for them at present but that he hoped to be back in the Government in a few months' time and would press for a stronger line on the North". Also, that he would "pass on anything he hears on that aspect but to keep his name out of it". That would seem to indicate that he would continue to keep them informed.

It was clear from this memorandum that Haughey was devious, could not be trusted, and was prepared to play both sides. Yet Jack Lynch, a short time later, made the extraordinary decision to allow him back on the front bench. At that time, Haughey was on the "chicken and chips" circuit, whipping up support among Fianna Fáil grassroot members all over the country for his return to the Cabinet.

Jack Lynch was conscious that Haughey, with a huge home base support in North Dublin, was almost certain to win a seat as an independent. He thought it was better to have him inside the Fianna Fáil tent, where he could keep a closer eye on him.

When Lynch subsequently brought Haughey back as Health spokesman, he was asked to explain his decision by two furious members of the front bench – George Colley and Jim Gibbons. Lynch told them: "I am preaching reconciliation in the North; I have to be seen as practising it in the south."

By the way, when Haughey met Joe Cahill, he was talking to the most powerful figure in the Provisional IRA, which was founded in late 1969. A member of the Provos' army council and its Belfast commander for many years, Cahill was involved in gun running from Libya, orchestrated by Colonel Gaddafi in 1972. The five-ton arsenal of weaponry on the Claudia was confiscated off the Irish coast and the six crew members, including Cahill, were later sentenced to three years' penal servitude. Cahill was released early from prison because of health difficulties. But it did not curtail his activities.

He next appeared in Boston, negotiating for another arms shipment with the notorious gangster James "Whitey" Bulger. During a brief chat, Whitey asked him how many British soldiers he had killed. Cahill smiled but did not reply. Subsequently, the crew of the gun-running American trawler Valhalla handed over the arms and ammunition to the Irish trawler Marita Ann off the Kerry coast. Kerry TD Martin Ferris, who was on board the Marita Ann, was subsequently sentenced for gun running.

During the peace process negotiations under John Hume and Gerry Adams, Cahill was deployed to sell it to key supporters in the United States. Authorities balked at allowing him in. It required the negotiating skills of Taoiseach Albert Reynolds to intercede with President Bill Clinton.

"Have you seen this man's record?" asked Clinton.

"Sure, there's no saints in the IRA," replied Reynolds.

*Frederick Forsyth: safe from kidnapping thanks to Haughey's request to the Provisional IRA.*

The visa was granted despite noisy protests from the British Government. Later, Cahill travelled to New York, where he performed his last significant service for the republican cause, signing up the US supporters to the peace process. Later, he received a standing ovation at the Sinn Féin conference in Dublin in 2003, when he told delegates: "We have won the war; now let us win the peace."

Haughey made further contacts with the IRA leadership in the late 1970s. This was to make representations on behalf of his new friend, spy novelist Frederick Forsyth.

The international best-seller had lived in Enniskerry, Co. Wicklow, for five years and had availed of Haughey's tax free status for writers. He was, however, under pressure from his wife to return to Britain because of the many kidnaps and the escalating troubles in the North. Haughey made a phone call to his friends on the Provos' army council, who assured him that Forsyth "would not be touched."

Haughey relayed the call to Forsyth and gave him a personal guarantee. When the writer rejected the assurance, he offered him another carrot – a seat in the Senate.

A few days later, Forsyth visited the Taoiseach and told him:" Look, I'm sorry, but we wish to leave and go back."

Later, Forsyth revealed that he was friends with Haughey even though the then Minister for Health was "never a friend of the United Kingdom." He said: "I don't know how or why we got on, but we did."

He added: "He had a lady friend at the time (Terry Keane] who used to give intimate little dinner parties around the pine table in her basement kitchen, to which my wife and I were invited. There were often only six or eight people there. That was when Charlie took his jacket off and relaxed a bit, had a few jars and became very affable and whatever. We got on well, I think."

The writer later revealed that Haughey asked him for advice on how to keep Pope John Paul II safe during his 1979 Papal visit.

Still in reconciliation mode in the Cabinet, Haughey wanted an uplifting coup to improve his ratings and his leadership chances within the Government. And the Forsyth paper on how to keep the Pope alive was the perfect answer. Haughey presented the detailed Forsyth memorandum to Cabinet – without revealing the name of the author.

## DÁIL SPY

Chatting with a number of colleagues in the Leinster House bar, I stumbled across a fascinating mystery man.

Sitting at the counter, he cleverly had his back to a delegation from the Palestine government. Having earlier met the Minister for Foreign Affairs, the delegation were sitting in an alcove in the corner talking with several Fianna Fáil members, including Mick Lanigan, the Limerick-born Senator representing Kilkenny.

I can reveal that the mystery man, who was by himself, was a journalist representing a British radio and TV network. I could see a tape recorder turned on and without a doubt he was recording the entire conversation of the Palestinian delegation.

Could he have been the Dáil spy who had been operating at Leinster House for more than twenty years without being outed?

# THE BULLY BOY

## HAUGHEY'S TAKE ON POLITICS

"Politics is not the boy scouts! It's a bit of a haul. And I think, per se, it has to be; you've got to sort of win your spurs and fight your way through ... It's a long hard haul; most of the guys who are at the top have served out a pretty tough, demanding apprenticeship ... I could instance a load of fuckers whose throats I'd cut and push over the nearest cliff, but there's no percentage in that. – Haughey in a 1984 interview with Hot Press.

## HAUGHEY AND THE SECRET COURTS

The story of Garda James Travers is a story of abuse of power by a government minister, interference and undermining of the democratic process by a member of the judiciary, and corruption at the highest level of the Gardaí. It also involves the then Minister for Justice, Charles Haughey, and the "secret courts" that he organised for Fianna Fáil VIPs.

Garda Travers, who had been based in Store Street, Dublin, was simply doing his job in the early sixties when he arrested a government minister who was driving the wrong way at Upper O'Connell Street and Cavendish Row. The minister in question, the flamboyant Donogh O'Malley, who was then a junior minister in Finance, had been involved in a late-night drinking session in Groome's Hotel, at the top of O'Connell Street. That was a favourite after hours drinking spot for politicians, actors, lawyers, journalists, and late-night shift workers from Dublin Airport.

The late fifties and early sixties were a dark, murky period for the Gardaí. That was when a garda had to be extremely careful doing his job. Unlike now, he had no effective union to protect him and, more importantly, he did not have the option of going to Europe with his grievance. In contrast, ministers had sweeping powers and exercised them without mercy.

The favourite taunt from a minister when questioned by a

POLITICAL BETRAYAL

*The Evening Mail reports on the Travers case: Garda Travers paid a price for arresting Donogh O'Malley.*

garda about a possible breach of the law was: "Would you like a pint or a transfer?"

O'Malley was stopped by Garda Travers for driving down the wrong way in a one-way street on March 13, 1962.

When stopped by Garda Travers, he was asked: "Did you not see the arrows?"

"I didn't even see the fucking Indians," was O'Malley's colourful reply.

Garda Travers then arrested him for drunken driving. As the court case approached, he was put under enormous pressure by his senior colleagues, who wanted him to drop the charges. At the same time, political strings were being pulled by O'Malley's great friend – the then Minister for Justice, Charles Haughey.

Garda Travers would soon encounter the notorious "Haughey secret courts" – which allowed Haughey, with the co-operation of a member of the judiciary and senior members of the gardaí, to hold a sitting of the District Court to facilitate errant members of Fianna Fáil in trouble with the law.

These courts sat early in the morning before reporters turned

# THE BULLY BOY

*Donogh O'Malley with his wife Hilda. "Arrows? I didn't even see the fucking Indians."*

up or they were held late in the evening when reporters rose with the daily sitting. A short time later, the judge would return to hear the case involving the Fianna Fáil VIP. Without the reporters present, there was no embarrassing publicity about the case.

This was, in effect, a blatant interference and undermining of the democratic process. It was also a breach of the constitution which protects the media.

The O'Malley sitting came under this magic spell. Again, the Judge stood up and the media left. A short time later, the judge returned to hear the case.

O'Malley pleaded guilty to drunken driving and was fined £25 and disqualified from driving for twelve months. The plan to evade publicity, however, was thwarted when *Evening Mail* editor John Healy was given details the next day of the case from a court official. The details were subsequently splashed on the front page of the paper.

O'Malley confronted Healy a week later: "Are you the fucker that crucified me in the Mail?" Healy indicated defiantly that he was, whereupon O'Malley invited him to have dinner with him the next night. While a great friendship over the years ensued between O'Malley and Healy, life became difficult for Garda James Travers.

With the subsequent widespread publicity of the case, the issue was raised in the Dáil by members of Fine Gael. It was stated that Garda Travers was given three days to resign from the force. He had refused to go on traffic control duty, claiming it was not his turn do so, since he had been on similar duty two weeks previously.

The penalty under the regulations at the time for refusing to go on point duty could be either a dismissal or a fine. In several previous cases, fines had been inflicted.

In the Dáil on July 17, Haughey answered a series of questions about the resignation of Garda Travers. He explained that five charges had been preferred against the garda, including one of discreditable conduct and disobedience of orders. On humanitarian grounds, he had been given the opportunity by the Commissioner to resign, according to Haughey.

Fine Gael's James Dillon asked: "Is not it a coincidence that this member of the garda was, in the course of his duty, associated with the prosecution of a member of the Government and immediately afterwards he was involved in this extraordinary story?"

Gerard Sweetman (FG) also asked: "Isn't this one of the most amazing coincidences that has ever occurred."

The Taoiseach, Sean Lemass (Haughey's father-in-law), replied: "That is a scandalous and most irresponsible statement to make." (One could ask the question – did Lemass know about the Secret Courts).

James Dillon said that there was a special duty on the Minister for Justice to clarify the situation and to make it manifest to the country that there was no connection between that and the voluntary resignation of the garda.

Haughey told the Dáil that it was a travesty to infer that the Garda authority would be a party to what had been suggested by Deputies Dillon and Richie Ryan.

When Richie Ryan asked if it was true that never in the history of the force had such punishment been meted out for a breach of discipline. "Was it not a fact that a fine or a transfer to a less attractive station had been the punishment in the past?"

Haughey said that this was a complete misrepresentation of the situation. The punishment, he said, was decided on by the Commissioner after Garda Travers had refused to do an ordinary detail and after he had refused to reconsider his attitude.

Richie Ryan asked the Minister whether it was the custom for members of the Garda Síochána concerned with prosecutions not to be present in court during the hearing of a case.

Haughey said that in the case in question the proceedings were conducted by the Chief State Solicitor's Office and that as the charge was not defended, it was not considered necessary, in accordance with practice, to have all witnesses in court. At the hearing, the superintendent of the district and the station sergeant who was the senior member directly concerned with the prosecution, were present.

Richie Ryan, who had earlier asked when the reign of terror in the Garda and in the Department would cease, then got to the nitty-gritty of the case... the fact that it was heard after the judge had risen and the media had left.

He asked if the Minister would state that a recent press report that a charge against a member of the Government was heard after the hour of 4 p.m. Was that report true?

Haughey said it was not true.

Asked what time the charge in question was heard, Haughey said it was heard between 3.30 and 4pm. He also denied that the court did not previously adjourn on that date and sit again after the press had left.

Ryan pressed Haughey further and asked if disciplinary proceedings would be taken against the court official who leaked the information of the case to a member of the media.

Haughey: "Perhaps you can advise me Ceann Comhairle, would the term 'political scavenger' be in order?"

Gerard Sweetman (FG): "If the Minister starts that line, we will perhaps ask questions about another garda who is also by amazing coincidence asked to leave."

Haughey: "There are some quare files in my office."

Dillon: "Let us not be pushed too far."

The widespread exposure of the O'Malley case ended the Haughey Secret Courts. Also, O'Malley received so much sympathy from his colleagues over the exposure that he vowed: "No bastard in a newspaper will ever get that chance again." Overnight, he stopped drinking, and continued to abstain until his sudden death in March 1968.

I put a number of questions to the Garda Press Office about the Travers case. I asked what were the full circumstances of his resignation? What part did the then Garda Commissioner and the then Minister for Justice, Charles Haughey, play in his resignation? I asked who was the Justice involved?

The Press Office replied: "Further to your discussion with Supt. John Ferris under data protection rules we are not permitted to proceed further on this matter without receiving the consent of former Garda Travers. Unfortunately An Garda Síochána have been unable to ascertain contact details for former Garda Travers and as a result are not in a position to provide any material relevant to your query."

The Travers case raises a number of issues, which need to be addressed by the current Minister for Justice:

- What were the full circumstances of the resignation of Garda Travers?
- Is the Minister aware that during Haughey's term as Minister for Justice secret courts were held to ensure there was no publicity for special Fianna Fáil members?

- Did the Secret Courts undermine the democratic process and breach the constitution?
- What part did a member of the judiciary play in the secret courts?
- What were the financial arrangements in respect of the retirement of Garda Travers?
- Did he receive a pension from the Garda Síochána?
- Were his family compensated by the Garda Síochána or the State for the disgraceful manner in which he was treated?

There is a public interest in finding the answer to these questions.

## THE POLITICS OF SURVIVAL

Haughey's survival through four leadership heaves is a testimony to his political astuteness. He was regarded as the most professional and adroit in Leinster House since Eamon de Valera. He knew exactly how to control a wavering TD. Sometimes he would get someone who had the means to put the maximum pressure on the TD in question or he would personally confront the TD and threaten him, usually in relation to some business deal. These methods were invariably successful.

The most notable challenge to him as leader of Fianna Fáil came when he was in opposition just weeks after losing the general election in December 1982. In January 1983, many of his hitherto faithful supporters including senior minister Albert Reynolds, told Haughey he must go. A substantial number of the Fianna Fáil National Executive, the ruling body of the party, also expressed a view that he should step down because the people in the constituencies were turning against him. Haughey sensed that as far as he was concerned, the game was up, but he told his parliamentary party: "If I go, the decision to go will be taken in my own time."

Former Dublin Lord Mayor and only Jewish member of the Dáil

*Jubilation as Haughey survives a vote against him in 1982 as party leader.*

Ben Briscoe put down a motion of "no confidence" in Haughey in February 1983. He then became worried after a disturbing call. The situation became so ugly that Briscoe was advised by Des O'Malley and by Assistant Garda Commissioner John Fleming that he should accept a police escort until the vote was taken. At home, he, his wife, Carol, and family fielded abusing phone calls, some of them expressing in no uncertain terms that it was a pity that Hitler had not "finished the job."

On the day of the vote, a Garda car escorted Ben Briscoe from his bungalow home in Celbridge, Co. Kildare, to Leinster House. But when he got there the chairman of the parliamentary party, Jim Tunney, – a loyal supporter of Haughey – surprised the members by adjourning the meeting because of the sudden death of Donegal TD Clem Coughlan, who incidentally had been opposed to Haughey. The ten-day adjournment gave Haughey and his loyal lieutenants desperately needed breathing space to work on the doubtful voters.

Forty-one TDs – a majority – had signed a petition calling for a party meeting to discuss Haughey's leadership.

Exerting enormous pressure, particularly in business deals, Haughey and his team managed to convince at least eight of them to change their minds. Haughey survived by 40 votes to 33. In that campaign, there were many "jumping heads" – as party Chief Whip Seamus Brennan called them. All of those who changed their vote succumbed to Haughey's carefully planned campaign and were subsequently rewarded with influential jobs and lucrative contracts.

Haughey's attention to every detail was the hallmark of his success. Before he attended any dinner function, he demanded to know who was on his right and left side and ordered brief profiles on those sitting closest to him.

There are many stories of Haughey's browbeating, bullyboy tactics. He had many stormy sessions with his first Government Press Secretary, Frank Dunlop, who had also acted for his predecessor, Jack Lynch. When Dunlop arrived in the Taoiseach's office one Monday morning Haughey was immediately confrontational. He shouted at Dunlop: "Where the fuck were you yesterday?"

Dunlop sarcastically replied: "Yesterday was Sunday, wasn't it?"

Haughey turned to the others at the meeting and said: "The bollox has a brain. He remembered it was Sunday."

As he stormed out of the meeting, Frank Dunlop shouted: "Don't ever talk to me like that!"

Haughey's genial political advisor, the late Pádraig Ó hAnracháin, ran after Frank Dunlop, saying: "You can't talk to the Taoiseach like that."

Dunlop countered: "You have it wrong, Padraig. He can't talk to me like that."

They did not meet for a week, but again Haughey apologised in a roundabout way by asking Frank Dunlop, in a sheepish voice, to come up to his office.

When he was Minister for Justice in the sixties, Haughey had a celebrated brush with the powerful secretary of the department, Peter Berry, a civil servant who had served with no less than thirteen Ministers for Justice during his long, celebrated career. They had a minor row about an appointment. And when the young Minister for Justice did not get his way, he threw the file on the floor. Berry stormed out of the office, leaving it there.

Deputies Sean Power and Sile de Valera also incurred Haughey's wrath by asking questions about reports in the "Backchat" column of the *Sunday Independent*. These referred to a private deal that he had negotiated with the newly elected independent Roscommon TD Tom Foxe. When they queried if the reports were accurate and if he could give details, Haughey gave them the "Mae West" treatment. "Call up and see me in my rooms," he said casually.

A couple of hours later when they arrived, he tore into them.

As he slammed the door, he asked: "How the fuck did you get past convention." The two bewildered and shocked TDs were taken back by the bitterness and venom in the Taoiseach's verbal assault.

A couple of years later, Sean Power used the Haughey attack effectively against him. In the last leadership crisis meeting in November 1991, three months before he resigned, Power, a bookmaker from Kildare and son of former Minister for Defence Paddy Power, reminded his colleagues of the "real" Haughey when he put him under pressure at the earlier meeting. At that November meeting, 22 deputies voted no confidence in Haughey. They included Albert Reynolds who was to succeed him, former European Commissioner Padraig Flynn, and the former Justice Minister Máire Geoghegan-Quinn. Haughey survived until the Sean Doherty bombshell two months later about more 'phone tapping charges and the devastating allegations from Dr. John O'Connell.

The Dublin North East TD Liam Fitzgerald also had some memorable clashes with his leader, including one in 1987 when Haughey effectively imposed his son Sean on the Fianna Fáil organisation. The three candidates selected – the former Minister for the Marine, Dr Michael Woods, the late Ned Brennan, and Liam Fitzgerald – had privately agreed that they would not back young Haughey, who had just completed a term as Lord Mayor of Dublin. To try and woo Fitzgerald, Haughey had three meetings with him. In the first, both exchanged earthy language and Haughey knew he could not change the attitude of the former Limerick-born teacher.

At a second meeting, Haughey turned on the charm. In his private study in Kinsealy, the family silver was displayed as Liam was invited to join him for tea. "Your potential has never been fully realised by the party," he told Fitzgerald. But his guest refused to accept his hospitality or his blandishments and stood during the entire meeting. In their third meeting, Haughey resorted to his old form – sustained barrack-room language – without success. Liam Fitzgerald, a formidable opponent, stormed out of his home, refusing to co-operate in any way. The upshot of it was that Sean Haughey failed in his election bid. But he was successful a couple of years later when Haughey resigned from his old constituency of Dublin North Central.

The worst case of bullying by Haughey came when he clashed with three Wicklow councillors and a solicitor. They had all been calling for his resignation. On a cold wintry day, all four were summoned to Kinsealy. They arrived at 8am and were not even offered a cup of tea. One by one he saw them. Three were persuaded to change their attitude, but the fourth, Wicklow solicitor Sean O'Brien, refused to change his mind and repeated that Haughey should step down. O'Brien, who was in a short list for a judgeship, came out of the meeting ashen faced. "I am dead, I am finished," he told his colleagues.

Shortly after this meeting, O'Brien, totally disillusioned with Haughey's dictatorial style, emigrated to Australia with his wife and

*They were long-time political allies, but Brian Lenihan was completely dominated by "The Boss".*

four young children. He saw no future in living in Ireland under Haughey's autocratic rule.

The undermining of Seamus Brennan was another classic Haughey move. Brennan had been General Secretary of Fianna Fáil and suggested to Cork businessman Barra Ó Tuama that they should commission an opinion poll to see what sort of support there would be for a new party. The result was very encouraging. It showed 25 per cent of voters were interested, so that Brennan was indirectly responsible for the establishment of the Des O'Malley-led Progressive Democrat party. Haughey knew that Seamus Brennan was influential in the growing anti-Haughey camp, so he removed him from all the internal Fianna Fáil committees – while he was still General Secretary. By cutting his power base, Brennan had no other option but to resign his post. But the episode opened up a new career for the Galway-born South Dublin politician who later became a successful Minister.

The bullying tactics used by Charles Haughey were not confined to TDs and party colleagues. He used the same tactics at Cabinet level. One Minister, Michael Woods, was reduced to tears at a Government meeting. Highly qualified, Woods interjected in a discussion, for Haughey to shout at him: "Who asked you to speak?" A couple of Ministers, including Albert Reynolds, challenged Haughey and told him he should never talk to a Cabinet colleague in that fashion.

One of Haughey's closest political friends was the late Brian Lenihan who, despite his formidable intellect, was completely dominated by Haughey. In 1982 when the Taoiseach and Lenihan, his Foreign Minister, attempted to move the formidable Sean Donnellan from his post as Irish Ambassador to Washington, Lenihan agreed to give me an off-the-record briefing. He greeted me in the magnificent surroundings of his plush office in Iveagh House in Stephen's Green and I assured him at the beginning that the meeting was completely off-the-record and none of what he said would be attributable to him. For fifteen minutes Brian Lenihan talked around the story without giving me any new information. In the middle of the meeting, he repeated: "This is off-the-record." I assured him it was. As he finished the meeting, having given me hardly anything, I again assured him that the meeting was off-the-record. I was halfway across Stephen's Green, on my way to Leinster House, when I heard somebody shouting: "Kevin, Kevin!" I looked around. It was an out of breath Foreign Minister. All he said was: "That was off-the-record", demonstrating how much he feared his leader.

Haughey also clashed with President Mary Robinson on several issues, mainly about the limits of her role. The former senator and senior counsel (and later United Nations representative on human rights) had promised to push out new frontiers during her presidency. But Haughey, who saw himself as the real President of Ireland – a bit like his friend President Mitterrand of France – attempted to limit her powers at every opportunity. He prevented her on occasions from doing interviews and curbed her travels abroad to give speeches on various topics. When she sought permission to do certain things, Haughey's response to many of her requests was: "It is not appropriate."

Journalists were also in his line of fire. At a briefing for political correspondents in New York, it was noticeable that the vibes were poor between Haughey and the then political correspondent of *The Irish Times*, the late Dick Walsh. Haughey pointedly asked Walsh why he never addressed him as Taoiseach. "Have you no respect for the office?" he asked. Walsh's reply was a classic. "It is because I have the utmost respect for the office of Taoiseach that I call you Mr Haughey."

## SENATOR TOLD TO JUMP

Fianna Fáil Senator Don Lydon, a psychologist at St John of God's Hospital in Stillorgan, Dublin, decided to offer some useful advice to Haughey as to why the party had lost a recent election. As he pinpointed some obvious mistakes, Haughey interrupted him with a growl: "Wait a minute; I don't want a fucking shrink to tell me why we lost the election. I want someone to tell me how we can win the next one. Fuck off out of here."

The leader's office is neatly panelled in pine. Lydon had difficulty finding the door. Haughey looked up from his desk to find the senator still there. He barked: "Are you still here?"

"I can't find the door," came the desperate reply.

Haughey replied "Well, then jump out the fucking window so!"

## OFFICIAL HUMILIATED

Haughey's most famous outburst was against one of his secretaries who had spent some time preparing a special report for him. Haughey summoned the official to his office. When he joined Haughey, he was ignored for a few moments.

Then Haughey stood up from his desk, flung the full report towards the official in temper and shouted: "Is that the best you can fucking do?"

The tall, well-built civil servant was totally crushed and humiliated. A few moments later, the humiliation changed to bubbling anger.

He coolly walked over to Haughey who was now sitting at his desk. He grabbed him by the lapels, pulled him close to him and shouted: "If you do that to me again, I'll fuck you out the window"! The official turned around, stormed out, slamming the door.

Haughey was totally surprised and shocked by this outburst. Still in a temper, he gathered up the pages of the controversial report, walked towards the window, opened it, and threw the pages out, watching them floating down the façade of Government Buildings.

## CLASH WITH LIAM LAWLOR

The clash between Haughey and Fianna Fáil TD Liam Lawlor was a classic and could be mistaken for a scene from "The Sopranos".

Haughey summoned Lawlor to a meeting in his office after he heard that he was about to defect to the new party – the Progressive Democrats, led by his arch enemy, Des O'Malley.

At the start, Haughey flattered him: "Liam, you and I go back a few years, both in sport and politics. During that time, you pulled off a few chancy deals and made a bit of money…and good luck to you."

Then he changed tone and got straight to the point: "Now, I have to ask you a straight question and I want a straight answer: Is it true you are thinking of defecting to O'Malley's crowd?"

Lawlor was shocked by Haughey's frankness. He replied: "Since you asked a direct question, I will give you a direct answer. I gave the matter some consideration. I believe O'Malley is a good party leader with the potential to be a future prime minister."

Haughey was taken aback by his frankness. "Do you now"?

POLITICAL BETRAYAL

Lawlor thought he had an advantage. "Yes, and I will go further. I believe that as a leader you're gone past it."

Haughey immediately stood up from his desk. "Gone past it, you say?" He walked over to his filing cabinet and took out a file. On the cover was the word "Confidential" and underneath … "Dublin County Council… Planning Applications Irregularities."

Haughey walked over and put the file on the desk in front of where Lawlor was standing. The file contained pictures of councillors taking bribes from businessman. The councillors were named.

Haughey: "Maybe you should have a look at that before making rash comments about your party leader."

Lawlor was puzzled and glanced at the files. He looked at Haughey: "What's this about? What has this to do with me"?

Haughey walked towards the window, his back turned to Lawlor. Staring out through the window, he spoke slowly and precisely.

Haughey: "It is a list of deputies and councillors in the Dublin area who took bribes from planning developers."

He continued: "You will see some pictures of them receiving brown envelopes. Those envelopes contained thousands of pounds. I am very concerned about it."

As he was talking, Lawlor glanced through the file, his face red with embarrassment.

Lawlor: "What's this got to do with me"?

Still looking out the window, Haughey replied: "Have a look at the file. What you want to see is under L."

Lawlor found the file and began to read a police report when a picture fell out on the floor. He picked it up. It was a picture of him being handed a small brown paper parcel by a well-known Dublin property developer. He recognised instantly the pub where the money was handed over.

Lawlor could not believe the next page of the file. It contained his bank statements from eighteen different banks in Europe and

America, showing more than €10 million in all his accounts. He opened the next page of the file. It contained a few pages of wire taps on him – clear evidence of him being compromised.

Haughey allowed him to study the file for a few moments and then he quickly grabbed it.

"The Minister for Justice has recommended that the file should be sent to the Director of Public Prosecutions. And there is also a recommendation that the Revenue Commissioners should be told. I'm inclined to agree with the Minister."

Lawlor was visibly shaking.

Haughey pressed home his advantage. "This is a shocking business. However, there may be other considerations, so I will not make a hasty decision.

"I will digest the contents for a couple of weeks, then let private investigators know what they should do with this information. As of this moment, my feeling is that I have a duty to hand this report over to the police and to the Revenue Commissioners."

Still shaking, Lawlor tried a last resort. "Look, there's no need to be hasty. We can work something out."

Haughey smiled, knowing he had broken Lawlor.

Haughey: "Sure we can. We must work out something to avoid bringing this scandal out into the open, don't we"?

The Taoiseach carefully put the two files back in his filing cabinet. He sat down behind the desk again.

"I know exactly what we're going to do. You are going to resign from the party and defect to O'Malley's 'Posh Democrats'. And then every week you will visit me and give me a full run down on what is happening in that organisation…. And I mean a full run down." He pressed home his advantage: "Do I make myself clear"?

Now cringing with embarrassment, Lawlor, barely heard, responded: "Yes. I understand what you are saying, and I am willing to co-operate."

Haughey was triumphant. "Oh, you'll do more than co-operate. You will be my eyes and ears inside that party."

Totally subdued, Lawlor whispered: "Yes. Your eyes and ears, every week."

As he was leaving, Haughey challenged him again: "By the way, what kind of a car do you drive?"

Lawlor responded: "The new Mercedes 8 series."

Haughey: "Get rid of it."

"But I am only after buying it. It costly me €80,000."

"I said get rid of the fucking thing. We can't have a gobshite driving around in a car bigger than the Taoiseach. Get rid of it."

Lawlor: "Yes, Taoiseach."

## RTÉ ENCOUNTER

Haughey liked to put chief executives in their place. When visiting RTÉ he was always met by the Director General of RTÉ. At one time, when Vincent Finn was DG, Haughey swept in and ignored him, making a big fuss over another Vincent (Scally), who oversaw hospitality. After a while, he turned to the DG and said: "Ah, Jesus, Finn, are you still here? I thought you were dead!"

## GEMMA'S 'BRUSH' WITH HAUGHEY

Former Education Minister Gemma Hussey had a brush with Haughey when she was a young, attractive Fine Gael Senator and Haughey was the Minister for Health.

She was so concerned about the new family planning legislation being enacted in 1977 that she sought a personal meeting with the new Minister. When she arrived for the meeting, he dismissed his official from his office in the Custom House. The young Senator began to outline her anxieties about the impending legislation when he interrupted her to say: "I don't think the Billings method would suit you or me."

A few years later when Hussey became a TD and Haughey became Taoiseach, he walked behind her in the Dáil gallery during a vote and began to playfully grope her and pull her bra strap.

Though in awe of the Taoiseach, she turned around and quickly put him in his place.

## A POLITICAL BURIAL

Haughey's duplicity in respect of the arms crisis was laid bare at a dramatic meeting of the Fianna Fáil parliamentary party back in 1981.

An article in *Magill* magazine was extremely critical of the role played by him in the illegal importation of arms. The then leader of the opposition, Garret FitzGerald, put down a motion in the Dáil condemning the role of Charles Haughey, who was then Taoiseach.

Haughey told a tense and packed party meeting that there would only be one speaker from Fianna Fáil in the subsequent Dáil debate and that was the then Minister for Justice, Gerry Collins.

Jack Lynch, who was still a member of the parliamentary party, rose to say that since his name was mentioned in the *Magill* article, he "intended to speak."

He was followed by the former Minister for Defence, Jim Gibbons, a central and controversial figure in the arms crisis, who had told his colleagues that he also intended to contribute. There was an eerie silence, with a couple of speakers weighing up their options. Eventually, a newly elected Senator from Galway, Jim Doolan, Professor of Business Studies at UCG and brother-in-law of Haughey's great political rival, George Colley, stood up to speak.

In a loud, clear voice he told a hushed meeting that since the issue raised by Garret FitzGerald touched on the integrity of the leader of Fianna Fáil – and by implication the Fianna Fáil party – he was surprised that the leader was not going to address the issue.

As he was posing the question, a quorum bell rang in the Dáil, which meant they had to return to the Chamber. The meeting ended abruptly, and the matter had to be dropped.

At the end of the meeting, Professor Doolan walked up from the back of the hall to the top table, where Haughey was standing. As he came closer, Haughey glared at his former accountancy colleague – Doolan had qualified as an accountant at the Haughey-Boland accountancy firm – and was heard to say that he had been watching him and did not like what he was seeing.

In an angry tone, he told the professor that he was "on a slippery slope" and had better watch his step. Doolan coolly replied: "That is a matter of opinion."

Doolan, who was a Fianna Fáil candidate in the 1979 European election, stood for the Senate on five subsequent occasions. Haughey had sent the word out that Doolan was to be "buried... politically speaking." Doolan never won a Seanad or European election seat while Haughey remained leader. But he did continue to speak out about "scandals", Haughey's "secret benefactors" and his "autocratic" leadership during his twelve years at the helm.

### THREATS TO A GARDA AND ARMY OFFICER

Two of the most damning events against Haughey in his long political career were his threat to the career of a young garda who was not "flexible" to his requirements and later implied threats to a young army officer when he was leader of the opposition.

When he was Minister for Justice in the early sixties, he became embroiled with a young garda, James Travers, leading indirectly to his early resignation from the force (see page 59). The second incident, involving a young army officer, came about twenty years later against the background of political manoeuvring by Haughey.

In 1982, the Garret FitzGerald-led coalition government collapsed when it attempted to tax children's shoes in the Budget. Independents Sean Dublin Bay Loftus and Jim Kemmy voted against the Government, which was defeated by one vote.

Haughey then called President Hillery to persuade him that there was no need to agree to a general election. Instead, he said, the President should refuse to dissolve the Dáil. As opposition leader, he was ready to take over and the move would spare the country millions.

Although Haughey later issued a blanket denial that either he or any of his party were involved in calls to the President, we have established that at least five calls were made on behalf of Haughey and at least two by Haughey himself.

The pressure calls were answered by a young Army officer on duty, Captain Ollie Barbour, who was ADC to the President.

Relentless pressure on him first came from Haughey's secretary, Catherine Butler. Next came a call from deputy leader Brian Lenihan, followed by Hillery's party colleague in Clare, Sylvester Barrett.

Hillery was successful in deflecting most of those who sought to exert pressure on him without great difficulty. Haughey was not so easily deterred.

According to the official biography of Patrick Hillery by John Walsh, the Fianna Fáil leader made his first call to the Áras at 8.15pm, announcing that he was available to form a government and wanted the President or his secretary to contact him. Haughey's message was direct and to the point: "I do not wish the Dáil to be dissolved."

Catherine Butler made a further call to reiterate Haughey's desire to speak to the President or his private secretary. She was informed by Captain Barbour that neither Hillery nor his private secretary were available. Both Brian Lenihan and Sylvester Barrett had no success in their attempt to talk to Hillery. Lenihan then made two further calls to check whether his and Haughey's messages had been passed on to the President. He was re-assured that they had been, but that the President was not available. (Ten years later, Lenihan, the then Presidential candidate, denied making the calls, and that denial cost him the election).

*President Hillery gave an assurance that a young army captain who stood up to Haughey would not be victimised.*

An impatient Haughey, at this stage, decided to turn up the heat. He declared his intention to call up to the Áras personally to see the President. Haughey's message to Captain Barbour was blunt and uncompromising: "I am leader of the largest party in the Dáil. I wish to speak to the President on a constitutional matter and it is urgent. I propose to call to the Áras at 22.00 hours to see the President. Please inform the President. I will wait for his answer."

Hillery stated in his biography: "When it got very hot and Haughey was threatening, I said 'Tell him I do not think it appropriate to speak to him'; that was the only message I delivered."

After Haughey – whose father was an army officer – won the subsequent election, Hillery took the unprecedented step of calling to the Army Chief of Staff, Louis Hogan to ensure that Captain Barbour's career was not affected by the affair. He told General Hogan that everything that was done, was done under his direct orders.

When Captain Barbour refused to put Haughey through to the President, Haughey requested his army number – generally regarded as an insult. Captain Barbour honoured the Haughey request.

Later, the Chief of Staff, a Clare man, assured the President that the young officer would be safe and that the President's words would be put on his record. Hillery ensured that the captain would be fully protected for playing his part in safeguarding the presidency on the 27th of January, 1982.

# MONEY MATTERS

## THE REAL STORY OF THE CARYSFORT DEAL

There were many audacious deals done during Haughey's term as Taoiseach and his twelve years as party leader. One deal that crept under the radar to a large extent was the sale of Carysfort College on the south side of Dublin.

The lands belonged to the Sisters of Mercy and were potentially of huge value if developed for housing. Planning permission for housing would, of course, be difficult. The nuns, facing a decline in vocations and the closure of the college, were anxious to sell at a reasonable price.

A group of developers – one from the North and two from the Republic – decided to take a chance on the lands and paid €2 million for the twenty-acre site. Their attempts to get planning permission failed. It appeared that they had gambled heavily and lost.

Enter shrewd businessman Pino Harris who had made a fortune importing Hino trucks from Japan and selling them in Ireland and Britain. The British market was especially lucrative for him because he could sell his imported trucks more cheaply than the English dealers.

Harris was a close friend and supporter of Haughey, who we now know was in contact with him about the potential of Carysfort. On the advice of Haughey, Harris bought the site and buildings for €6.25 million, providing a handsome profit for the original investors. Pino had been persuaded by Haughey that it was possible to turn the college into a private third level institution, attracting students from the US, the Middle East, and from Ireland.

It was ironic that the Government had an opportunity to purchase Carysfort six months earlier and expressed no interest in it.

But after Haughey became involved, events moved swiftly.

Strangely, civil servants were excluded from the discussions between Haughey as Taoiseach, the then Minister for Education, Mary O'Rourke, and Dr Paddy Masterson, the UCD President. No fewer than eight private meetings took place between the three. But for Masterson's forthright testimony later to the Dáil Committee on Public Accounts, much of what happened might never have come to light. At an informal government meeting on December 4, ministers agreed that their education and finance colleagues should consider the use of the college as a school for business management, with possible support from the state. Two weeks later, the Department of Finance under Albert Reynolds agreed that a supplementary estimate for €9.7 million would be put before the Dáil for the purchase of Carysfort. But not only was the Department of Finance unhappy about the price being paid; its jealously guarded constitutional right to be consulted had been ignored.

Reynolds stipulated that the new business college should be self-financing with no subsidy for its running costs from either the State or UCD. But Masterson had already made it clear to Haughey and O'Rourke that the proposed school would need continuing support.

The supplementary estimate put before the Dáil included the €8 million purchase price and a further €1.7 million to help UCD prepare the building and set up the school. In six months, Pino Harris had cleared a profit of €1.75 million. And the kick-back to his friend Charles Haughey for masterminding the whole deal – a cool half million!

Considering that Mary O'Rourke was fully involved with her leader in this dramatic deal, you would have thought she might have something to say about it later.

In her 233-page memoir, *Just Mary*, she chose to ignore the highly irregular deal, which cost the taxpayers almost €10 million. There was not a mention of it in her biography.

During the negotiations, the Department of Finance and the Minister, Albert Reynolds were not consulted. Their right to be consulted was ignored by Haughey and his Minister.

Later, Albert Reynolds checked with Frank Murray, Secretary to the Government about whether or not it was a Government decision that Carysfort would be sold to UCD. Frank Murray told him it was not a Government decision. The decision was made by the Taoiseach and Mary O'Rourke.

## MYSTERY OF TANGLED FINANCES

The mystery of the tangled finances of Charles Haughey deepened after his and his wife's will were revealed.

According to documents lodged in the Probate Office in Dublin, he left an estate valued at €1,029,955. But after deductions for debts and funeral expenses the net value of his estate was €930, 012, which he left to his widow, Maureen.

When Maureen died on March 17, 2017, she left more than €9 million. According to her will, she left the contents of her home and all her personal belongings to her daughter, Eimear, with the residue of her estate to be divided among her four children, Eimear, Conor, Ciaran, and Sean.

This is all puzzling and just does not add up, considering that Haughey received €45 million in 2003 when he sold the Kinsealy estate to Joe Moran's Manor Park Homes. And according to the Moriarty Tribunal, he received €45 million (in today's money) throughout his political career from big business to finance his lavish lifestyle.

That lifestyle included spending – according to the Tribunal – IR£26,000 per month on wining, dining and presents for mistress, Terry Keane and IR£16,000 a year on Charvet shirts and suits from Paris.

One of the biggest scandals of his thirty-five years in politics came when he was Minister for Finance. In November 1967, when the Irish pound was linked to sterling, the Government was given twenty-four hours' notice of a devaluation by the Harold Wilson

Labour government. In a brazen, shameful move, Haughey decided to use this privileged information for his own benefit and to pass on the information to a small group of businessmen, who made a quick financial killing. Haughey's personal turn of fortune allowed him to purchase a 130-acre stud farm in Ratoath, Co. Meath, a year later without having to borrow. The whole affair was later investigated by the Revenue Commissioners, but strangely the Moriarty Tribunal was precluded from inquiring into the transaction. Over the years, Haughey "touched" these businessmen when he required millions to finance his lavish lifestyle. They became his "Golden Circle."

Despite all his backhanders and "dig-outs", however, he owed AIB €1.4 million when he became Taoiseach in December 1979. During his twelve years as Taoiseach, he regularly contacted the "Golden Circle" and tapped them on a constant basis to help finance his extravagant lifestyle.

Some years later, a Cabinet colleague disclosed that Haughey was "on the inside" with architect Sam Stephenson who designed the Central Bank building on Dame Street, Dublin, and also designed a special bar in Haughey's Abbeville home called "The Snug." He told several of his friends that Haughey insisted on a percentage of every Government contract that Stephenson won. The money was lodged to Haughey's Cayman Islands account.

We know now that the former Taoiseach had substantial interests in the renovation of the Temple Bar area in central Dublin, which he compared to the Left Bank in Paris. Apparently, he had a financial interest in several apartments between Parliament Street and Christ Church Cathedral.

The abuse of the passports-for-sale scheme (see "His biggest earner" on page 128), which eventually led to his resignation in 1992 after he was exposed by former Ceann Comhairle John O'Connell, was probably the biggest earner for Haughey. The passports scheme allowed rich Arabs to collect Irish passports once they invested a

*Abbeyville: an eighteenth-century mansion on 250 acres.*

minimum of €1 million in Irish companies.

O'Connell knew most of Haughey's benefactors, in particular Saudi billionaires who had contributed substantial sums to the former Taoiseach. O'Connell bluntly told Haughey in 1992 at a meeting in Kinsealy that he would expose him at a special press conference – unless he received his letter of resignation.

Back in 1959, just two years after he was elected to the Dáil, Haughey bought a property in Raheny in north Dublin for IR£10,000. He later sold it for IR£200,000. And in 1969, he bought the eighteenth-century Abbeville in Kinsealy on grounds of 250 acres for a massive sum at that time – R£120,000. Most of the burden of the purchase was offset when he immediately sold seventeen acres of the estate to Roadstone.

He also bought summer homes in Wexford and Sligo before purchasing Inishvickillane island off Dingle in Co. Kerry in 1975 for IR£20,000. It is now worth more than €2 million.

Although he accumulated substantial property, we now know

that Haughey was in dire financial straits when he became Taoiseach in December 1979. His Cabinet colleague George Colley told me at that time that he had an overdraft of IR£1 million with AIB (confirmed later by the Tribunal). The bank denied the story at that time to the Evening Press.

In fact, he owed AIB IR£1.4 million after he succeeded Jack Lynch as Taoiseach. He later settled the AIB account for a fraction of what he owed. AIB forgave Haughey £400,000 of the debt after he warned them: "I can be a very troublesome adversary."

In a settlement with the Revenue Commissioners in 2003, Haughey handed over €6.28 million. By that stage, he had sold off cash-rich land around Kinsealy. In 2001, nine acres were sold to Treasury Holdings for €7.6 million.

But the big deal came two years later when he sold 230 acres to property developers Manor Park for around €45 million.

Over an eighteen-year period while leader of Fianna Fáil and Taoiseach, he received a total of €45 million in today's money from big business, according to the Moriarty Tribunal. But we know now that he received much more than that – approximately €70 million.

The revelation that was most damaging to him and helped to open the financial can of worms that led to the Moriarty Tribunal was that former supermarket supremo Ben Dunne gave him IR£250,000 in bank drafts and a cheque for IR£1.3 million, for which Haughey's immortal reply was "Thanks a million, big fellow."

But the most harmful revelation of all and the one that did the most damage within Fianna Fáil was when he organised a fund-raising drive in 1989 for Brian Lenihan's transplant operation at the Mayo Clinic in the US. The Moriarty Tribunal examined this in detail and found that during a five-week period in May and June some £336,000 was raised for the operation, but just £88,000 was required. Haughey ordered his senior officials to divert the balance to his Fianna Fáil leader's account – almost £250,000. It later transpired

*Lord of the Manor: at home in Abbeyville.*

that £200 was handed in an envelope by Haughey's driver to Ann Lenihan, wife of Brian Lenihan.

No investigation has been held by Fianna Fáil as to what happened the missing £250,000. It was never properly explained by

Haughey, who at that time denied any impropriety on his behalf.

The question remains: whatever happened to the estimated €70 million given to Haughey by big business throughout his career and the €45 million cheque presented to him when he sold Kinsealy in 2003.

We know he had a lavish lifestyle. On top of his lavish dinners and expensive gifts to Terry Keane, as well as the huge amount spent on Charvet shirts and suits, there were also his art collection, his vintage wine cellar, his antiques for Abbeville, and of course the purchase of his yacht, Celtic Mist, and his stud farm at Kinsealy.

His settlement with the Revenue in 2003 means his family will not have to worry about demands from the tax man. It is estimated that his three sons, Conor, Ciaran, and Sean, and daughter Eimear inherited substantial amounts from their parents in properties and shares.

The only member of his family who was required to declare his interests was former Lord Mayor of Dublin and twice Minister of State, Sean Haughey. He was named in a *Sunday Independent* poll as the fourth wealthiest TD, believed to be worth €4.8 million, with property worth €2.45 million and pension values of €1.5 million – none of which includes a share in his mother's €9 million will or his father's massive legacy. In the latest *Irish Independent* rich list, published in September, 2021, Sean Haughey is again named as the fourth richest TD. His share holdings and pension pot were again named as worth €4.8m. His diverse portfolio included shares in Pfizer, Amazon, and Walt Disney.

The mystery of Haughey's wealth has been compounded by the fact that files in the Land Registry relating to the various lands owned by him have not always been available for public inspection. Many of the original files were deliberately kept out of circulation for years, and some are still not available. That is a common trend throughout Haughey's political career. Also, most of the Haughey files on the arms trial are missing, as is the Garda file on the famous "fall from a horse" story.

The last word must go to the Moriarty Tribunal, which said that the scale and secretive nature of the payments to Haughey by big business "can only be said to have devalued the quality of a modern democracy."

## REGULAR VISITORS TO KINSEALY

Regular visitors to Kinsealy were: Dermot Desmond, the billionaire businessman, the late Des Traynor, Haughey's financial advisor, Michael Smurfit, owner of the K Club, and Larry Goodman, the beef baron and now the owner of two private Irish hospitals. They visited mainly on Saturday.

Apparently, Haughey tried to pin down Tony O'Reilly a couple of times without success. His comment on the former Indo boss was: "He is a guy who invites you to lunch but always forgets the date."

## A FINANCIAL KILLING

The dramatic intervention in a multi-billion telephone deal of Albert Reynolds when he was a minister is explained for the first time.

Over a cup of coffee in the hospitality tent at the Irish Derby more than a year before he died, Albert Reynolds revealed to me his detailed knowledge of a deal behind new multi-billion digital telephone system introduced to Ireland in the early 1980s.

At that time, he was Minister for Posts and Telegraphs and was aware that Haughey was in secret negotiations with his close friend, President Mitterrand of France. The controversial discussions were being held at Haughey's private island in Inishvickillane in Co. Kerry.

Reynolds told me that he was "disturbed" by rumours circulating in Government circles that Haughey was about to make a "financial killing" in the new telephone deal. Through his officials, he learned that Haughey wanted to give the entire multi-billion deal to France.

"As the line Minister, I decided to intervene," Reynolds told me. The Government was also negotiating with a Japanese company, and he insisted on bringing Sweden into the talks. The result of his intervention was that France got 60% of the multi-billion deal and Sweden received 40%. He revealed that he believed that Haughey received a substantial financial kick-back from Mitterrand for orchestrating the deal.

Reynolds' statement confirmed an interview I had before this with George Colley, who told me that Haughey had received a considerable sum from the French for the deal.

At that time, a secret agreement was also signed with the US Department of Defence, which ensured that the new digital equipment conformed to normal civilian standards. The agreement with the Pentagon ensured that Ireland's new digital network would be able to carry the Pentagon's new Joint Tactical Information Distribution System. Also, at that time, a new digital link was provided from Dublin to a Ministry of Defence radio station at Slieve Croob, six miles north-east of Banbridge, Co. Down.

## HIS BIGGEST EARNER

The biggest earner for Charles Haughey was the passport investment scheme run in the 1990s by the Fianna Fáil government.

One scheme, involving an Arab sheikh, resulted in a lucrative €3 million payment by a middleman to Haughey when he was Taoiseach.

Official documents suggest that Haughey personally handed the passports over to eleven people – eight Saudi Arabians and three Pakistanis – at a lunch in the Shelbourne Hotel. The passports were given as part of the passports-for-investment scheme, in return for a promised £20 million sterling investment programme in Ireland by Sheikh Khalid bin Mahfouz, the owner of Saudi Arabia's only private bank and one of the kingdom's wealthiest men.

According to sources in the Department of Justice, the then Minister for Justice, Ray Burke, did not press the Mahfouz passport application. But his action in signing the certificates on Saturday, December 8, 1990 has continued to generate political controversy as details of the saga have dribbled out over the years.

Worry over how and why the eleven passports were issued caused Burke's successor in justice, Maire Geoghegan-Quinn, to order an internal inquiry.

The Mahfouz affair began on August 20, 1990 when a firm of English solicitors, Mitchell and Co., based in Suffolk, wrote directly to Ray Burke at the Department of Justice, referring to an extremely wealthy Arab gentlemen with royal connections "who could make an immediate investment in the country of £100 million sterling."

Three days later the solicitors again wrote to Burke, fully identifying their client, Sheikh Khalid bin Mahfouz. Their note read: "We have indicated to you that the Sheikh is extremely interested in rapidly ascertaining whether or not a waiver of the normal rules governing an application for citizenship can be applied in his case. We believe that it is maybe in your country's interest in this case to grant special treatment because of the financial investment that this gentleman could make in your country".

To his credit, Burke refused to meet representatives of Sheikh Khalid but he did arrange for them to be put in contact with the Industrial Development Authority (IDA), which was the standard practice at the time.

Meanwhile, the promised investment of £100 million was considerably reduced. On the day the passports were issued, a letter to the Department from Patrick Kenny of Haughey Boland and signed by Sheikh Mahfouz confirmed the availability of £20 million sterling for suitable commercial concerns in Ireland.

With the sheikh and his party scheduled to arrive by private jet in Dublin for the Shelbourne lunch, Ray Burke signed the naturalisation orders. This was a highly unorthodox action. Normally, naturalisation certificates are signed by a senior official, usually an assistant secretary with the delegated authority of the Minister.

In October 1994, Fine Gael's Gay Mitchell put down a Dáil question about the circumstances in which the passports were granted. Although the question was not reached, the then Minister for Justice, Máire Geoghegan-Quinn ordered an assistant secretary in her department to review the case.

Later the minister stated: "I have read the file very carefully and I have to say I am very concerned and alarmed about its contents." She went on to describe the details of the case as "highly unusual to say the least" and to note that details about the promised investment were "extraordinarily scanty by any standards."

She added: "I have some very serious concerns about the granting of naturalisation to the eleven persons in this case. If full, thorough, and satisfactory answers to these concerns are not available, I am of the view that the certificates of naturalisation should, if possible, be revoked in each of the eleven cases. "

In January 1995, Dermot Cole, the assistant secretary requested by Geoghegan-Quinn to investigate the affair, reported his findings to her successor, Nora Owen. The report found that Burke's decision to sign the naturalisation orders ran contrary to standard procedures in the department.

"It is the invariable practice, except in the case of honorary citizenship or a celebrity figure, for certificates to be signed at official level." The inquiry also found that it had been possible to account through the IDA for only £3 million of the £20 million sterling. There was no trace of the other promised £17 million.

It is interesting that only £3 million of the £20 million has been traced – the exact amount pocketed by Haughey, according to a former close associate of his, Albert Reynolds.

MONEY MATTERS

## TRIBUNALS LEAVE REPUTATION IN TATTERS

In February 1997, the McCracken Tribunal was set up to investigate alleged secret payments by Ben Dunne to Charles Haughey and to former Fine Gael Minister Michael Lowry. The tribunal reported later that year that Haughey's evidence under oath was untrue and that Lowry had, with Dunne's assistance, evaded tax. In the wake of these findings and the revelation of substantial funds in secret Ansbacher accounts, the government set up the Moriarty Tribunal to investigate more fully the financial affairs of the two politicians.

For a long time, the tribunal team of solicitors, officials, accountants, junior and senior counsel were inundated with documents. They included bank statements, cheques and numerous notes covering detailed memoranda. And the probe was further complicated by letters and statements in special codes.

Against this background, a journalist had written that supermarket tycoon Ben Dunne had given a one million gift to a politician. At that time, it was not known who the politician could have been. The financial conundrum appeared to be extremely difficult for the officials.

Then the sensational breakthrough came. It was a simple handwritten note at the end of hundreds of letters. A junior member of the team spotted the significance of the note written to Des Traynor, the man who controlled Haughey's finances.

The writing was that of Joan Williams, secretary to Des Traynor. The note concerned the withdrawal of £25,000 sterling from one of the coded accounts. The sensational and dramatic document for the Moriarty team read: "By hand to CJH 30th of November, 1993." The CJH had to be Charles J. Haughey. The official spotted that this was the only document bearing Haughey's name in the thousands of documents. The tribunal official had also discovered the reference HC opposite two other accounts. HC was obviously "Haughey Charles."

The junior official confided with his senior colleagues. They were confident that they had broken the complicated and intricate code and smashed the elaborate Ansbacher banking system Haughey had used to secretly fund his lifestyle. The officials were confident that a financial noose was slowly tightening on the former Taoiseach.

In essence, the banking system was simplicity itself. But it was so designed as to be surrounded by a near-impenetrable wall of secrecy. Haughey's personal secretary in Kinsealy would send the bills to a company called BEL Services. Jack Stakelum, an accountant who did his articles under Haughey in the firm of Haughey Boland, ran this company. Stakelum got the money through Guinness & Mahon bank and later Irish Intercontinental Bank and paid the bills. But the ultimate source of the money was the so-called "Ansbacher" accounts in the Cayman Islands.

This system was operated by Padraig Colleary, a banking software expert who, at the time, was an associate director of Guinness and Mahon. In the late 1980s, the Ansbacher accounts in the Caymans held almost £38 million, belonging to a variety of individuals, including a number of Irish politicians.

Subsequently, Colleary was confronted by the Tribunal with the dramatic note referring to CJH and later admitted he handled accounts for Haughey and explained to the Tribunal about the management of his expenses.

When the tribunal reconvened, counsel Denis McCullough disclosed the existence of the Ansbacher Deposits and coded memorandum accounts and the fact that some of those accounts held funds belonging to Haughey. He revealed that the money from the deposits paid for Haughey's expensive lifestyle.

 He further disclosed that the Tribunal team had proof that some of the money from supermarket tycoon Ben Dunne to Haughey had been used to pay off a loan the former Taoiseach had with the Agricultural Credit Corporation bank. He then declared that Haughey had received the £1.3 million gift from Ben Dunne.

Haughey's counsel, Eoin McGonigal, then announced that Haughey accepted "as a matter of probability" that he had indeed received the £1.3 million. Haughey denied that he had not been personally aware he had got the money, but his limited admission was sensational.

Subsequently, Mr Justice McCracken ruled that Ben Dunne's solicitor Noel Smyth should disclose the contents of his eight different meetings with Haughey in Kinsealy, at Smyth's home and at a friend's house. Smyth was outlining matters connected with his handling of Dunne's legal affairs when he casually mentioned communications between himself and Haughey. Smyth had discussed with Haughey the payments the Tribunal were investigating. Smyth said he would not divulge the contents of the conversations unless directed by the court to do so.

At a subsequent meeting, Haughey was sounding out Noel Smyth on a number of issues. He wanted to know what Ben Dunne's attitude would be if he was called before a Dáil committee to answer questions about alleged payments to politicians. Smyth told Haughey that he believed Ben Dunne would wish to avoid giving evidence but if called he would appear.

Noel Smyth said he had written a statement concerning the Haughey conversations and posted it to himself. He had it with him in a sealed envelope. Mr Justice McCracken ordered that the envelope be sent unopened to Haughey's home in Abbeyville and adjourned the hearing.

Subsequently, an order of discovery was made against Smyth for his telephone logs covering his conversations with Haughey. When they were examined, the team found several calls from Haughey in 1994. When asked about these, Smyth revealed that he had first discussed the Dunne payments with Haughey in 1994. A second series of conversations had occurred in 1997.

This was sensational new evidence. The effect of Smyth's further statement was that Haughey could no longer maintain that he had not being aware of the payments. Haughey later filed a new statement saying he had known of the payments since 1993. Haughey further added that he now accepted he had received the three Dunne bank drafts for €210,000 in 1991 when he was Taoiseach. He said he had no recollection of the payments but he accepted Ben Dunne's version of events.

This revealed that Haughey had lied persistently to the tribunal, causing the State and the taxpayers considerable expense and bringing disgrace upon himself and his family.

When Haughey accepted that he received the three Dunne cheques for €210,000 he was admitting that he received a large personal donation from a businessman while holding the most powerful office in the State.

Also, when Haughey finally appeared before the Tribunal, he admitted that he had not paid any attention to his financial affairs since the 1960's, leaving them to his colleague and friend, Des Traynor, so that he could get on with running the State.

On his way out of Dublin Castle, he waved to the large crowd who threw – in a biblical gesture – thirty pieces of silver at him and booed him continuously until his car drove off.

Haughey's reputation was utterly demolished when the long-awaited Moriarty Tribunal report found that he had corruptly accepted an astonishing total of £11.6 million in clandestine payments, equivalent to €45 million today.

Rejecting all his justifications, the 700-page report found the scale and highly secretive nature of the payments from senior business people to Haughey – at a time he was championing austerity – "devalued the quality of a modern democracy."

The one thing Haughey will never be forgiven for is pocketing money intended for the liver operation in the United States of his friend Brian Lenihan. Mr Justice Moriarty described the transfer of vast sums of money – as much as £190,000 – as "reprehensible." The report says that Haughey kept on raising money even though the ceiling had already been reached.

The judge found that a £50,000 payment made by Saudi Arabian diplomat Mahmoud Fustok was in return for passports received by his family.

And in one of the gravest conclusions, he concludes that in return for payments of almost £2 million, Haughey intervened improperly in Ben Dunne's tax problems by arranging meetings with the then chairman of the Revenue Commissioners, Seamus Paircéir. Dunne's tax bill was subsequently changed from £39 million to £16 million.

The tribunal rejected almost all Haughey's claims and specifically found as "unbelievable" his contention he was unaware of any of the arrangements made by his financial adviser Des Traynor.

The shredding of Haughey's reputation stands in marked contrast to the eulogy delivered by Taoiseach Bertie Ahern at his graveside, when he said that history would judge him favourably. Ahern was also criticised for signing blank cheques for Haughey when he was party treasurer.

The Haughey family denounced the report, describing the findings in relation to Fustok and Ben Dunne as "perverse". Ben Dunne called the Moriarty Tribunal a "kangaroo court".

Opposition leaders described the reports findings as a damning indictment of Mr Haughey and a documentary on corruption in Irish politics. The Tribunal has done the State some service by issuing these impressive findings. It was important to find out the extent of the corruption. We now have some idea of it.

In June 2012, the first ever corruption and bribery law reforms were brought for approval to the then Minister for Justice and Equality, Fine Gael's Alan Shatter. Some of the new proposed laws include: prison sentences of up to ten years and unlimited fines on any member of government or civil servant who commits an act of corruption.

## AN UNSOLVED MYSTERY

One mystery remains unsolved about Charles Haughey. When his close friend, the Minister for Education, Donogh O'Malley died in 1968 Haughey drove to Limerick to sympathise with the O'Malley family. The only person in the house at the time was Donogh's son, Daragh who was then 15.

After a few minutes, Haughey, then Minister for Finance, made an unusual request. He asked if Daragh had access to the keys of the safe. Daragh produced the keys and Haughey immediately opened it and removed several documents. Haughey gave no explanation to the young O'Malley for this. At the time there was speculation that the two Ministers were tied up in some business deals. And this provided further speculation that Haughey might have had leverage over him financially.

Daragh O'Malley, now a prominent and successful actor, was summoned to Kinsealy by Haughey a couple of months before he died back in 2006. According to Daragh, they never discussed what was in the documents, and Haughey never explained why he removed them.

## FOOD FAVOURS

A close friend of mine was walking near the Bank of Ireland in Dame Street, Dublin, when he spotted an associate of his leaving the bank. Over coffee, the acquaintance told my friend that he was on his way to Kinsealy…with a case full of cash. He emphasised that the money (a half million) was for Haughey. It was a gift from his boss for political favours rendered. The associate told my friend that over the years the multi-millionaire food executive had paid Haughey more than €5 million for political favours.

# HOW IT ALL CAME TO AN END

## HOW IT ALL CAME TO AN END

### DR JOHN OUT-MANOEUVRES HAUGHEY

During his twelve years at the helm of Fianna Fáil, four heaves were organised against Haughey. The first was in October 1982 when Charlie McCreevy put down a motion of no confidence in his leader. The coup failed after only twenty-two TDs, including three ministers – Des O'Malley, George Colley, and Martin O'Donoughue – voted with McCreevy. The "Twenty-Two Club" was born.

When the last coup was organised in November 1991 twenty-two also voted against Haughey, but he won the contest comfortably. That twenty-two included the country and western alliance leaders – Albert Reynolds, Padraig Flynn, Maire Geoghegan-Quinn, Michael Smith, and Noel Treacy. On a bitterly cold November evening a couple of weeks later, the plot to unseat Haughey was hatched. A group of former Ministers were determined to win the next contest. And they were confident they would succeed without a contest.

*The winds of change....*

In the Athlone home of Sean Fallon, the former Cathaoirleach, the downfall of Haughey was planned in detail, and it was decided to adopt a two-pronged attack.

At the time, Sean Doherty, the former Minister for Justice, was in the political wilderness after Michael Noonan, as Justice Minister in January 1983, revealed that he had unlawfully tapped the phones of journalists Bruce Arnold and Geraldine Kennedy. What Noonan did not reveal was the extent of unofficial tapping organised by Doherty. It was widespread and included several TDs, Senators and journalists. For ten years Doherty remained in political limbo. But to close friends, he had always revealed that he had a "can of worms" that would seriously damage Haughey.

At the secret Athlone meeting, Doherty was persuaded to deliver his "Haughey knew about the phone taps" speech. But Doherty did not come cheap. He was almost bankrupt at the time. The Irish Nationwide Building Society had issued a writ against him for repossession of his Cootehall house and brought him to the Circuit Court in Boyle. The outstanding arrears, spread over four years, were £35,000.

Around the same time, Doherty, who was Cathaoirleach of the Senate, had to pay Senator David Norris £6,000 following a legal row in the Senate. And the former Justice Minister also sustained a legal loss following a High Court case against *The Sunday Times*.

Miraculously, all his debts were cleared. How was this done?

I can reveal that at the meeting a fund-raising committee was launched. It was headed by the late Peter Hanley, who owned Hanley Meats in Rooskey, Co. Roscommon. Hanley had also impeccable Fianna Fáil connections and was particularly close to Brian Lenihan and Albert Reynolds. He was twice appointed Chairman of Aer Rianta. He also spearheaded the campaign to provide funds for Brian Lenihan's costly liver transplant operation – an event that brought serious opprobrium on Haughey when it was disclosed at the Moriarty tribunal that he kept a substantial portion of the fund-raising funds for himself.

The anti-Haughey businessmen had the money in place so that

## HOW IT ALL CAME TO AN END

Doherty could clear all his debts. That allowed him to deliver his part of the bargain – to detonate the phone-tap bombshell, which he did in late January, 1992. Then he told the media that Haughey knew all about the phone tapping of journalists ten years previously – a fact that Haughey denied.

For several years, Haughey was concerned that his former Minister for Justice, Sean Doherty, would disclose Cabinet details of the tapping of journalists' phones in the Haughey-led government of 1982. Doherty had been hinting that he was prepared to "blow the lid" on the whole affair. Haughey's loyal lieutenant and deputy leader, Brian Lenihan, was dispatched to Roscommon to try to persuade Doherty to keep quiet. Lenihan had a special rendezvous with Doherty on his boat in Carrick-on-Shannon. Over drinks and coffee, they spoke for a couple of hours. But the mission was unsuccessful. Doherty bluntly told Lenihan that he was ready to tell the full story about what happened in 1982... unless he was immediately re-instated into the Fianna Fáil party. Doherty, at that time, was in the parliamentary wilderness, having been forced to resign from the party over the phone-tapping affair.

Haughey was preparing for a trip to Libya to meet Colonel Gaddafi. He told his deputy leader, Lenihan to call a meeting of the parliamentary party and re-instate Doherty during his absence. In that way, Haughey could distance himself from the whole affair. Doherty was re-instated at that party meeting. And though he huffed and puffed, he kept quiet about the 1982 government – until he called a press conference in the Montrose Hotel in Dublin on Tuesday, January 21, 1992. In a bombshell announcement, Doherty revealed damaging details of Haughey's involvement in the phone tapping of journalists in his minority government of 1982.

In a tense-filled voice he read from a prepared statement, with his wife, Maura, sitting beside him. She was there to continue reading the statement in the event of Doherty breaking down.

His opening paragraph said it all. "I am confirming that the Taoiseach, Mr Haughey, was fully aware in 1982 that two journalists' phones were being tapped and that he at no stage expressed a reservation about this action."

Unveiling damaging details on the crisis-ridden Haughey led government of 1982, Doherty revealed that between March and November 1982, there were a number of serious leaks from the Cabinet which generated considerable concern within the Government. It was the function of the Minister for Justice, he said, to take steps to prevent such leaks. He sought the advice of the Deputy Garda Commissioner, Joe Ainsworth, who recommended the option of tapping Irish Independent political journalist Bruce Arnold and journalist Geraldine Kennedy, who would become the political correspondent and, later editor, of *The Irish Times*.

Doherty added: "As soon as the transcripts from the taps became available, I took them personally to Mr Haughey in his office and left them in his possession."

Anticipating an immediate denial by Haughey, he went into more detail: "I understand that the Taoiseach has already denied that this happened, so I wish to reiterate it in specific terms. Ainsworth forwarded to me the transcripts relevant to the Cabinet leaks problem. Each and every one of those relevant transcripts were transported by me to Mr Haughey's office and handed to him directly. He retained all but one of them, making no comment on their content. At no stage did he indicate disapproval of the action which had been taken."

The dramatic Doherty press conference was followed the next day by a brilliant rebuttal by Haughey at a hurriedly called news conference. But the problem with his performance was that no one believed him!

The then Taoiseach categorically denied the claims by Doherty and strongly refuted allegations that he had seen or been given transcripts

## HOW IT ALL CAME TO AN END

*Dr John O'Connell: snubbed by Haughey, but he got his revenge.*

of the phone-taps.

"I wish to state categorically that I was not aware at the time of the tapping of these telephones and that I was not given and did not see any transcripts of the conversations." He added: "I also wish to say that I have always abhorred the principle of phone-tapping except where absolutely necessary to prevent serious crime or subversion by paramilitary organisations."

But the Taoiseach was not to know that the coup to unseat him would be a twin attack – with Dr John O'Connell, who was appointed as Ceann Comhairle by Haughey in 1982, playing a hugely significant role, assisted by wealthy businessman and Fianna Fáil activist, Dermot O'Leary.

### TWIN ATTACK TO UNSEAT HAUGHEY

O'Connell, a wealthy doctor who had founded the Irish Medical Times, had originally been elected as a TD for Labour but left the party in 1981 when he was passed over for a Cabinet post in the coalition government of Fine Gael and Labour. He then became an independent and subsequently joined Fianna Fáil in the mid-1980s.

There is a fascinating background to O'Connell's role in the push against Haughey, which I can exclusively reveal now.

It all began when he was on a weekend break in Paris. Staying in the same hotel was the Saudi bloodstock dealer and billionaire, Mahmoud Fustok, who became ill while he was there. The hotel management called for a doctor and John O'Connell appeared. The two men subsequently became friends, O'Connell later becoming Fustok's personal physician.

Fustok later rang O'Connell with a strange request – to have his mares serviced by the National Stud. The problem was that there was a substantial wait of over two years, but this was easily solved when O'Connell rang Haughey, and Fustok was able to jump the queue.

This was a huge favour that Fustok did not forget. O'Connell acted as a conduit in 1985 for a £IR50,000 (€63,000 euro) payment from Fustok to Charles Haughey on February 18, 1985. Haughey had asked for the cheque to be made payable to "cash". The Taoiseach subsequently arranged for Lebanese nationals associated with Fustok to get Irish passports. Fustok later said that the money was in return for a horse. Haughey said the same in evidence to the Moriarty Tribunal (which later decided it was a corrupt payment).

Later, the Saudi billionaire, at O'Connell's request, organised the visit to Ireland of Crown Prince Abdullah of Saudi Arabia. A private dinner was held in Haughey's residence in Kinsealy, overseen by restaurateur Johnny Opperman. The Crown Prince subsequently sent two guns worth £30,000 each as a Christmas present to Haughey and a diamond necklace valued at £250,000 to Maureen Haughey. Most of Haughey's then Cabinet attended the magnificent banquet. But the Taoiseach never invited John O'Connell, the man who was responsible indirectly for the Crown Prince's visit. That turned out to be the biggest mistake of Haughey's 35-year career and subsequently led to his resignation.

The relationship between O'Connell and Haughey subsequently soured. Having decided "to wait in the long grass," O'Connell's moment came after Sean Doherty revealed all about the phone-tapping at an emotional press conference in the Montrose Hotel, Dublin, in January, 1992.

In February 1992, O'Connell and Dermot O'Leary sought a

meeting with Haughey. O'Connell advised Haughey that he could not promise to keep secret the details of his financial dealings with the wealthy Arabs. When the meeting was concluding, he produced a list of demands – which included a call for Haughey's resignation in writing.

Haughey, in total shock, pleaded for time. He told O'Connell to "come back at three o'clock to-morrow and I will give you an answer." O'Connell returned the following day promptly at the appointed time – and got a letter from Haughey, giving the date of his resignation. O'Connell immediately sought a meeting with Albert Reynolds, who was flabbergasted when he saw the letter. His response delighted O'Connell: "I think you would make a very good Minister for Health."

O'Connell lasted only eleven months as Minister for Health in the Albert Reynolds-led government. At the time, he was resented by several Fianna Fáil Ministers. O'Connell resigned his Dáil seat on February 24, 1993, on health grounds and spent his last few years between his plush apartment in London and his two luxurious apartments in Boca Raton in south Florida.

## FINAL DAYS AS TAOISEACH

It had been a traumatic, tear-filled week for Charles J. Haughey. On Tuesday morning, February 11, 1992, he was still Taoiseach and the most powerful man in the country. A couple of hours later, he was a mere backbencher, adrift, like most of his former cabinet colleagues, stripped of his title, his power and literally his office. He had arrived punctually at 9.30 a.m. in his showcase Merrion Street office, with its adjoining dining-room, sitting-room, bathroom, and kitchen. An hour later in the Dáil chamber, he formally announced his resignation as leader of the government. He talked of the "deep affection for this House and its traditions" that he had developed over his thirty-five years as a TD. In the VIP section of the Dáil gallery overhead, tears glistened on the cheeks of his daughter, Eimear, as she listened to her father's farewell speech.

Passing on the baton to his successor, Albert Reynolds, he quoted from Shakespeare's Othello: "I have done the state some service; they know't. No more of that."

If he appeared measured and controlled in the Dáil chamber on Tuesday, it was because he was emotionally spent. It was particularly touching to see all his old colleagues from every party wish him "bon voyage." A week of departing from the uppermost echelons of politics had proved to be interminable.

A fortnight previously, he announced his "lonely decision" to the Fianna Fáil parliamentary party in the big room on the fifth floor of Leinster House. The following night, shortly after 9 p.m., when celebrations for his son Ciaran's wedding were getting into full swing at Abbeyville, a couple of the guests became tearful at the prospect of the Taoiseach's retirement. He turned to them and chided: "Don't be sad. I'm not. I'm relieved."

A week before he retired, school children had been calling to the gates of Government Buildings with bunches of daffodils. Inside, the secretarial staff made small bundles of the St. Christopher medals arriving for "The Boss" from all over the country. Every message and letter were left on the Taoiseach's desk "so that he would know how much he'll be missed", explained a member of his staff later. She added: "It's been incredible. Every single senior civil servant wrote him a personal letter saying goodbye. As far as I know, that is unprecedented."

There were messages from world leaders. They included: George Bush, Brian Mulrooney, Bob Hawke ("there is life after politics"), Senator Edward Kennedy, and the 72-year-old Italian prime minister, Giulio Andreotti, who once made the famous remark: "Power ruins whoever does not possess it."

Monday, February 10, was one of the hardest days of all for

## HOW IT ALL CAME TO AN END

*The long goodbye: leaving Leinster House after his resignation as Taoiseach.*

Haughey. There were presentations by his private staff. They included: his private secretary, Donagh Morgan, his special advisor, Eileen Foy, his personal secretary, Catherine Butler, his Northern Ireland advisor, Dr Martin Mansergh and his arts advisor, Tony Cronin. According to his staff, they powdered him up and dried his eyes for his meeting with John Hume, who had become leader of the SDLP a month before Charles Haughey won the Fianna Fáil race in December, 1979. He came to thank him on behalf of the party "for everything he had done to keep Northern Ireland high on the political agenda." He also thanked him for the courteousness and openness he had always shown himself and he said that a lot of people in Northern Ireland "had talked to him about how they would miss Mr Haughey." After an emotional John Hume left, Peter Cassells, general secretary of the Irish Congress of Trade Unions and a key negotiator in the Government-union talks, called to the Taoiseach's office to bid him farewell on behalf of the country's trade unions.

Next it was the turn of the entire Department of the Taoiseach to give their goodbyes. Among the 200 or so who filled the conference room of the second floor of Government Buildings were the then Attorney General, Harry Whelehan, the Secretary to the Government, Dermot Nally, the Secretary to the Department of the Taoiseach, Pádraig Ó hUiginn, the staff from Abbeyville and the Taoiseach's wife, Maureen Haughey, who was visibly moved by the emotion in the room. The staff presented their departing Boss with a two-volume first edition (1791) of Francis Grose's *The Antiquities of Ireland*. Maureen Haughey was presented with an 18-carat gold Celtic brooch – a replica of one of the treasures in the National Museum – and a bouquet of her favourite flowers, lilies.

While a tearful Pádraig Ó hUiginn escorted Maureen Haughey back to her car, the cleaning staff of the Taoiseach's department – who had waited two hours for their turn – presented Haughey with a mass bouquet. That was followed by a special moment for his official drivers, Max Webster and Bobby O'Brien. After nearly a half century between them of driving "The Boss" around the country, they posed for their first and last photograph with him in the office of the Taoiseach. Haughey had been particularly generous to the two policemen. He had changed the retirement age of gardaí to ensure a

## HOW IT ALL CAME TO AN END

*A once faithful servant: Albert Reynolds hands his leader a cup of coffee, watched by Brian Lenihan and Michael Woods.*

couple of years extra for his drivers. And he also looked after their families when jobs were needed. Because of the guaranteed overtime by working for him, they were among the highest paid policemen in the force.

At 2pm on that day, Haughey travelled the short distance over to Fianna Fáil headquarters in Mount Street for yet another farewell party, hosted by the general secretary, Pat Farrell. The staff presented him with a silver salver from the Armada collection, made by Sleater's jewellers in Johnson's Court. Standing under the imposing portrait of Eamon de Valera, Haughey spoke of the "momentous decisions" that had been taken there over the years. He recalled having been in that room with all three of Fianna Fáil's previous leaders, Eamon de Valera, Sean Lemass, and Jack Lynch. And he mentioned the "frenzy" that filled the room during general election counts when he used to leave Mount Street for the RTÉ studios to accept either victory or defeat during his twelve years at the helm.

After a meeting with the incoming Taoiseach, Albert Reynolds, back in his office on Monday afternoon to discuss the hand-over of government leadership, Haughey made the journey to Áras an Uachtaráin at 5pm to inform President Mary Robinson that he intended to formally announce his retirement from the office of the

Taoiseach in the Dáil the following day.

That night, twenty of his closest advisors, friends, and family, including his loyal media guru, P. J. Mara, his devoted and courteous private secretary, Catherine Butler, his solicitor and long-time friend, Pat O'Connor, and his political buddy Brian Lenihan, his former Tánaiste, gathered in Abbeyville for a private drinks party. The cabinet had already presented him with a piece of George III silver, organised by Ray Burke, Mary O'Rourke, and Gerry Collins.

By Tuesday, February 11, his office in Government buildings had been cleared of all his effects, including his two favourite paintings, Paul Henry's "Connemara" and Nathaniel Hone's "St Doughlough's Church."

His children, Eimear, Conor, and Sean (Ciaran was still on his three-week honeymoon in Singapore) were already in the Public Gallery when he entered the chamber. Maureen Haughey had decided not to attend on the grounds that it was a day for the Reynolds family. But she joined her husband, her children, her son-in-law and daughters-in-law and Government press secretary P. J. Mara for lunch in the private dining room of Le Coq Hardi – a restaurant with cherished and abiding memories for Haughey and for his long-time mistress, Terry Keane.

Afterwards, Haughey returned to his office in Government Building. And shortly before the Dáil resumed at 3.30 p.m., he left his office for the last time as Taoiseach. As he walked through the glass tunnel connecting Government buildings to Leinster House, seven Gardaí and five uniformed ushers stood in line to salute him.

Sitting in the back of the chamber, he listened to Albert Reynolds read out the names of the new Cabinet. He was surprised to learn that eight of his former Cabinet were sacked by the new Taoiseach. When he left the chamber at 6.30 p.m., he had no office. Accompanied by P. J. Mara, Catherine Butler, and Donagh Morgan, he took the lift to the fourth floor and Brian Lenihan's office. It was poignant and ironic. After all their years as the numbers one and two in the government, here were the newly retired Taoiseach and the Tánaiste he had sacked more than a year previously, talking nostalgically about old times.

Haughey was looking forward to his retirement, not realising that a drama was about to unfold 3,000 miles away that would have a powerful impact on him, his family, and the nation.

## HIGH DRAMA ON THE 17TH FLOOR

It was a typically clear morning in March in tropical Florida when a sheriff's deputy, Ed Wright, was cruising in his police car. An attempted suicide call broke the silence at exactly 9.13 a.m. on Thursday, March 20th, 1992.

The call came from the Hyatt Regency Grand Cypress Hotel, a 1,500-acre resort just 18 miles from Orlando Airport and within two miles of the Disney World complex.

Nearby, Chicago-born deputy Stan Spanich had finished his coffee break and had just climbed into his police car when he also heard the call. Stan had been working the area around Disney World

Nine minutes later, Wright and another officer, Stan Spanich, who had heard the call, arrived almost simultaneously at hotel to meet a distressed female executive shouting that somebody on the seventeenth floor was attempting suicide.

The officers jumped on the elevator. As they raced from the lift, they saw on the corridor the tall figure of a big man, hands in the air in a v-shape as if about to dive into the gathering crowd underneath. He was screaming and calling for the police. At the same time, he was shouting to the two officers, "Get away! Get away!"

Stan Spanich, an experienced counsellor, began to talk to him. "What's the problem? Are you okay?"

The agitated man screamed: "I am surrounded; keep them away." He was getting closer to the railings, his hands still in the air.

Stan tried to re-assure him and win his confidence, while Officer Wright hid in a passageway so that he could not be seen from the balcony.

Stan asked the man his name. In a soft voice, the big man replied: "Ben."

The officer volunteered "I am Stan."

A bit calmer now, the man said: "I go by my first name." He casually mentioned that he was in the textile business. Stan responded: "That must be interesting."

Stan asked him if he was married. He said he was.

Again attempting to assuage his fears and win his confidence, Deputy Stan told him he had two girls, nine and eight, and a six-year-old boy.

Ben responded that he had a couple of kids too.

Stan assured him that he did not want anything to happen to him.

Desperately trying to get his mind off his suicide mission, Stan asked him the ages of his children. Later he casually asked him if he wanted a drink.

The deputy did not know that the big Irishman he was trying to coax down from the balcony was one of Ireland's top businessmen, supermarket boss Ben Dunne. He had no way of knowing, either, that Dunne had gone through a horrendous experience in 1981 when he was kidnapped by the IRA and held prisoner for a full week before escaping in the middle of the night by jumping into an open grave in a cemetery along the border with Northern Ireland. He had been held for seven days with a hood over his head and said later that he felt like "a caged animal" in constant fear of being shot.

They were talking for about forty minutes when Stan suggested that they should go back to his room where they could "relax a little bit".

Still agitated and foaming at the mouth, Ben repeated: "They are going to hurt me."

In a determined voice, Stan responded: "I will guarantee you I will be with you until this is all over." As he said it, Stan raised his hand as if swearing.

That seemed to strike a re-assuring chord with the big Irishman. Ben, now less agitated, responded: "If I get out of this, I will take care of you. If you guarantee me safety out of the country, I will take care of you." He then offered the police officer some money.

Stan immediately responded: "That is not necessary. That is my job."

Stan was beside Ben Dunne and began to walk towards his room. As they entered the hallway, Officer Wright and another detective who had been lying in hiding nearby jumped on him and handcuffed him.

Stan kept re-assuring him: "They are not going to hurt you."

The detectives searched for ID. In the right front pocket of his trousers a zip locked bag containing a white substance was found. It turned out to be cocaine.

Detective Chris Ford who arrived at the Grand Cypress just after his unformed colleagues Wright and Spanich, interviewed a witness, Denise Marie Wojcik. She said she was a prostitute hired by Dunne for the night. She said that she and an associate, Sherri, arrived at the resort around 10 p.m. the previous night. She told them she had seen Dunne using a large quantity of cocaine.

In an interview later with the *Sun* newspaper, Wojcik revealed how she and Ben Dunne snorted cocaine. In her lurid account, she described how they had taken part in a seven-hour cocaine-sniffing session, sprinkling lines of the drug on to the rim of the sunken Jacuzzi and inhaling it through rolled up $100 bills. But Dunne began acting strangely, she said, when he couldn't open the bedroom safe. She said that they discussed sex, but she told Dunne that none of the girls in her agency had sex with a client.

The big Irishman was put on a stretcher and taken to Sand

Lake Hospital by ambulance for possible cocaine overdose. At the hospital, Ben lost control again. Reliving his IRA nightmare, he shouted, with his hands in the air: "They are going to hurt me." He refused to let anyone touch him until Stan said: "It is going to be okay. I will be here with you all the time." He was treated and cleared medically. A few minutes later, the officers started to walk him towards the police car. Ben shouted again: "They are going to hurt me.". He began struggling and was handcuffed and shackled in a "hog-tie position" – handcuffs and feetcuffs joined together with a nylon tie. The officers had to forcibly push him inside the police car. Deputy Stan sat beside him and constantly tried to re-assure him as they drove to the Orange County jail police station, where Ben was charged.

Almost three months later to the day, his case came up at Orange County Circuit Court. It was dealt with in just over ten minutes. In an unusual concession, the court permitted Dunne to speak by telephone from Dublin and plead his defence. A charge of trafficking cocaine was dropped after his defence successfully argued that the search of the room at the hotel was illegal. The court decided that he would have to undergo a 28-day drugs treatment course in the Charter Clinic in Chelsea, London, and pay a $5,000 fine together with State costs of $700. There were other stipulations. He was required to be available for at least twelve months for aftercare that involved regular monitoring of his condition. That was to be organised by his Dublin lawyer, Noel Smyth. He was also to abstain from alcohol for a year. If he failed to comply with the court's rulings, he would be banned permanently from entering the United States. At the court hearing, his US visa was withdrawn.

The court sanctions from this wild escapade were minuscule, however, compared to the pending fall-out on his business empire and the effect that was to have not only on his own future within the huge family business, but also upon friends to whom he had been more than generous with company funds. And the man who was to suffer most of all was Charles Haughey, whom he had rescued from dire financial straits with huge donations of cash. (See "Tribunals leave reputation in tatters" on page 131.)

## HOW MY STORY ABOUT DOHERTY WAS SPIKED

I recall that Haughey-led Government of 1982 vividly. It cost me a three-week suspension from the Sunday Independent.

I got a tip-off from a highly placed senior Garda source that Sean Doherty's home county of Roscommon was worth a full-scale investigation. I was told to talk to the gardaí in the region – in particular, Sergeant Tom Tully of Boyle.

In his bungalow home on the outskirts of Boyle, Tom Tully, a quiet-spoken, fearless officer, told me about what he described as the "unbearable" political interference from Doherty and about the Minister's attempt to transfer him for doing his job.

The attempt to transfer Sergeant Tully failed because of the intervention of the then deputy Garda Commissioner, Larry Wren. At the special hearing to decide on whether Tully should be transferred, Wren voted with the Garda Sergeants and Inspectors organisation representative, Derek Nally, not to transfer Tully. Limerick-born Wren was later berated by Doherty for taking this courageous action.

Tom Tully's detailed story of political interference was followed by similar tales from five other gardaí who gave me signed statements on the extent of Doherty's interference. And in the event of Doherty suing, they were prepared to give testimony in court. The Minister for Justice, apparently, was doing everything but administering justice.

I returned to Dublin and asked to speak to the former Tánaiste, the late George Colley. I met him in his Leinster House office. When I entered, he locked both doors and took the two telephones off the hook.

*Sean Doherty: accused by garda officer of "unbearable" political interference.*

He amplified certain points in the story and pleaded with me to give him a copy of the signed garda statements for a specially called meeting of the Fianna Fáil parliamentary party the next day. Kildare deputy Charlie McCreevy (later the Minister for Finance and European Commissioner) had put down a motion of no confidence in Charlie Haughey.

"This could be dynamite at this meeting", Colley said. However, I refused the request, saying that I did not want to get embroiled in internal Fianna Fáil problems. Anyway, I said, the Sunday Independent would publish the story on the coming Sunday.

On Wednesday, October 13, 1982, twenty-two Fianna Fáil deputies, including George Colley and Ministers Des O'Malley and Dr Martin O'Donoghue voted no confidence in Charles Haughey. But he won the vote by a sizable majority.

I now know that Charles Haughey called a special meeting in Kinsealy the next day to consider what should be done about my story that was about to appear. A government Minister, Albert Reynolds, was instructed to contact my then editor, the late Michael Hand, to spike the story. Hand, who had not seen the copy at that time, agreed to the request.

On Friday, October 15, I had arranged to meet a high-ranking Garda contact about the Doherty story. A message was delivered to me at my desk in the *Sunday Independent* from the secretary of the senior garda. It stated that I should ring him – but not from my office 'phone. What he had to say was startling: my phone was being tapped; I was being followed; every effort would be made to keep my story out of the paper; and "the highest person in the country" knew what I had.

One of my immediate problems was that I had arranged a lunchtime appointment with a Fianna Fáil Minister who was giving me inside details on the Roscommon affair.

I walked out the back entrance of the Independent in Middle Abbey Street and was joined by a colleague, Paul Murphy, who would later become Editor of the *Drogheda Independent*. I asked Paul to walk with me for a few minutes – "but don't ask me what it is all about." We walked into Woolworths in Henry Street, left through a side entrance, and then headed up Henry Street towards O'Connell Street. Paul left me as I entered a side entrance of Clery's, took a couple of lifts to the second and third floor and later left through a back entrance.

Thinking that everything was clear and that no one had followed me, I entered the Abbey Mooney pub, where I spotted the Minister drinking at the counter. I beckoned him to follow me downstairs to the toilet. There, behind a closed toilet door, I unfolded my Doherty revelations. The Minister was extremely helpful. He amplified certain areas and we parted about thirty minutes later.

After returning to the office, I spent about three hours going through line-for-line my draft of the story with solicitor Michael O'Mahony. Michael changed about four words in the entire story. I was so delighted that I sought to meet Michael Hand in the Oval Bar around 7 p.m. to tell him we got legal clearance. Michael's reply sent out ominous signals. He had not seen the story at this stage, but he did say: "I think we will hold the story, but I will talk to you about it tomorrow."

On the following day, I showed the story to Michael Hand at 3pm. He called me back to his office at 4.30 and in the presence of his deputy, Michael Denieffe, told me that he could not use the story. He said that I was "crucifying" the Minister on flimsy evidence. I replied that the evidence was not flimsy and that the five gardaí were prepared to testify in court in the event of Doherty suing us. We argued for over an hour, with Michael Denieffe helpfully suggesting certain amendments, to which I agreed. Hand refused to agree to the amendments. And when I suggested that there were several follow-up stories to be investigated, he said to put them all into one story, "one big exposé."

Recalling the senior garda's warning that "every effort will be made to keep the story out of the paper", I spoke in measured terms to Hand. I told him that I was considering my position as News Editor and thinking of resigning. I said that I would find it impossible to work with him again.

I left the office at 6.30pm and made my way to the Fine Gael Ard Fheis in the RDS. Senior members of Fine Gael approached me and asked me if it was true that we were running a big story on Doherty. I refused to confirm the story.

An hour later, I was so frustrated that I decided to 'phone the proprietor of Independent Newspapers, Dr Tony O'Reilly, then the President and Chief Executive of H. J. Heinz. From a neighbour's house at around 10pm, I rang Pittsburgh. I outlined what had happened over the past week. When I said we had received legal clearance to run the story, O'Reilly asked me to repeat that. I did. He suggested that I should contact the Group Chief Executive of Independent Newspapers, Bartle Pitcher and make a case to him. The last thing O'Reilly said to me was: "I will respect your confidence on this."

I later discovered that O'Reilly was also contacted by the Fine Gael leader, Garret FitzGerald, who had been briefed by the general secretary of the Association of Garda Sergeants and Inspectors, Derek

Nally. And later I learned from the *Sunday Independent* political correspondent, Joe O'Malley, that he had established the authenticity of my story through independent sources. He told Michael Hand this and added that on foot of its publication further individuals would come forward with additional information.

On Sunday, I spent three hours with Bartle Pitcher who asked me to leave the draft of the story and all the back-up material. That night I left on a journalistic golf trip to Liverpool. It was a good time to get out of the country, I felt. And when I returned the following Wednesday, there was an urgent message from a colleague, John Devine, later the Northern Editor of Independent Newspapers. He said: "Be careful when you come into work. Hand knows you have been on to O'Reilly."

When I arrived at the office, Hand immediately summoned me to his office. He said that he wanted to talk to me, but first I had to see Joe Hayes, the Managing Director, Ireland, and then Bartle Pitcher. Within two minutes, I faced Joe Hayes who was immediately confrontational, shouting at me from his desk about ten yards away. Initially totally supportive of Michael Hand, he opened up the discussion by saying that if Michael Hand had used that story he would have immediately called for his resignation. I asked him to explain the back-up evidence from the police, which I had in my possession. All of them, I said, had given written undertakings to testify in court on our behalf. Then I informed him that the story was cleared legally to run. He was surprised at this and immediately changed his attitude, sitting beside me and putting an arm on my shoulder.

"What I am concerned about," he said in an assuring tone, "is your relationship with Michael Hand. How can you work together?" I told him that I had no confidence in Michael Hand and would find it extremely difficult to work with him.

I left the office of Joe Hayes and went to see Bartle Pitcher, who was a thorough gentleman, expressing his concern for what happened and telling me that he would consider using the story. I asked him if he had any objection to me giving the story to another newspaper in the event of Independent Newspapers not using it. He replied: "Yes, I have. You are an employee of Independent Newspapers."

A few minutes later, I was in the office of Michael Hand, who immediately told me that by getting on to O'Reilly I had undermined his position. He said that I had been totally "disloyal" to him. I told him that I had vehemently disagreed with his decision not to use the story and as a senior executive of the company I had every right to go over his head.

"Yes" he countered, "but you went over four heads to get to O'Reilly." He told me that I was off the story and that I was suspended as News Editor "until further notice".

For three weeks, I remained an outcast. The management certainly did not want to know me, and just a few colleagues spoke to me. They included Joe O'Malley, Frank Khan, and Kevin Moore, the father of the chapel of the National Union of Journalists. They were totally supportive. As far as management were concerned, I had committed a cardinal sin. I had spoken to the head honcho, over the heads of four senior executives. They were angry.

Meanwhile, a general election had been called. *Newsweek*, *The Sunday Times*, and several English papers begged me to give them the story. I refused. But when I sought advice from Kevin Moore, he told me to give it to RTÉ. Helpfully, he argued that they were not a rival newspaper. Three weeks later, RTÉ carried the story in a programme called "The Roscommon File." And this was despite more political interference. Another Government Minister, John Wilson, contacted senior executives in RTÉ to kill the programme. To their credit, they rejected his request. "The Roscommon File" was presented by the former Euro MEP Pat Cox, produced by Michael Heaney and edited by Joe Mulholland, later the head of RTÉ Television. The following day, an RTÉ journalist rang Michael Denieffe to tell him how "helpful" I had been in making the programme. A couple of months later, Michael Hand lost his job as editor. I was writing a political column called "Backchat" and also doing the difficult job of News Editor. I was told by the new editor, Aengus Fanning, that I could not hold on to both jobs. I opted to resign as News Editor and write the column.

A year after the television programme, I got a curious call from a Revenue official. He asked me why I had not included the fee I received from RTÉ in my earnings for the previous year. I told him there was a valid reason – I had not received any fee as I had told RTÉ I did not want one, but just wanted the story published.

One garda that I met in Roscommon back in October 1982 was Sergeant Dan Sullivan who was attached to Ballyforan. During the brief interview, he was paranoid. We were alone in a large lounge, and whenever a car passed, he would immediately stop talking and check if the occupants were coming into the pub.

What he told me was of paramount significance. The gardaí in Roscommon were afraid to do their job because of political interference and before issuing a summons they had to find out if the people concerned were members of Fianna Fáil. He told me that he was injured in an accident while on duty in Donegal in 1970 and had not received any compensation. Sean Doherty at one stage told him that he was going to be transferred, "so I should pack my bags." Because of that he was hesitant to do his job. He did not want to be transferred. His immediate superiors were friends of Sean Doherty, so he decided to contact the Taoiseach about the problem.

"I spoke to Mr Haughey on the telephone at his home. I told him that I was dissatisfied with Mr Doherty's interference and outlined what had happened." He also told Haughey that he believed that his phone was tapped and that there was widespread phone-tapping in the constituency.

Haughey told him he "did not want to know about it." According to another Fianna Fáil Minister, Haughey told Sergeant Sullivan to "outline his complaints in writing."

The fact that Sergeant Sullivan contacted Haughey at that time to tell him of Doherty's political interference with the Roscommon gardaí and of widespread phone tapping is of major significance. Haughey subsequently denied that he knew anything about journalists' phones being tapped in 1982 and strongly refuted allegations that he had seen or been given transcripts of the taps by the former Minister for Justice.

I believe Sergeant Sullivan's version of events – that Haughey was briefed by him as to what was happening. I also believe that Sean Doherty was telling the truth when he made that bombshell announcement in January 1992. Haughey kept in touch with his Ministers on a regular basis and was fully informed of what was happening in each department. He had to know what was going on in the most sensitive department of all – that of Justice.

There is one other factor that verifies Sean Doherty's version of events. When the Minister for Justice leaves the country on holidays, the Government is required to have him or her replaced. During his term as Taoiseach, the temporary duties of Minister for Justice were mostly taken over by Haughey. Thus, when Doherty left for France in August 1982, he had immediate access to all police and department files, including those on phone tapping. At that time, journalists Bruce Arnold and Geraldine Kennedy were officially tapped by the Government.

Politicians who believed they were being tapped along with Bruce Arnold and Geraldine Kennedy included Ministers Des O'Malley and Martin O'Donoghue, Roscommon-born Minister of State Terry Leyden, Fianna Fáil TD Ben Briscoe, a former Lord Mayor of Dublin, and George Colley, Haughey's former classmate.

Before I leave 1982, I should tell you that I kept a complete dossier on my own personal problems with the *Sunday Independent* and on my three-week investigation in Roscommon. The file included a copy of the story spiked by Michael Hand. The opening couple of paragraphs read:

> The Minister for Justice Sean Doherty has been involved in widespread interference with the administration of Justice – in particular in the Roscommon area.
>
> A *Sunday Independent* investigation over the last three weeks has revealed that he: "squared" a late drinking prosecution against a publican in Boyle; instructed a Garda not to post a sample in a drunk driving case; and harassed gardaí who were conscientiously doing their job.
>
> One garda disclosed that he was afraid of doing his duty "because of the threat of being transferred."
>
> In the drunken driving case in June 1981 involving a lady motorist, Mr Doherty was then a Junior Minister for Justice. He directed the garda involved not to post the sample. The member concerned told Mr Doherty that Sergeant Tom Tully of Boyle was involved in the case. The Minister's reply was "Tom is sound."
>
> Sergeant Tully instructed a garda to post the sample and requested that Mr Doherty be informed that any further contact on the matter should be made with himself. Sergeant Tully was not contacted subsequently by Mr Doherty. The case went to court and the lady was convicted and disqualified from driving.

Some years before the Haughey revelations, Sean Doherty had serious financial problems. Irish Nationwide Building Society took a case against him for non-payment of his mortgage. The case was settled on the doorstep of Boyle court. He had his house and a marina he owned at Cootehall marina up for sale.

After Haughey was deposed, Doherty's financial affairs changed dramatically. According to the Dáil manifesto, he owned land at Knocknacarrow, Cootehall, Boyle, which he let out. He was given planning permission by Roscommon County Council to build three two-storey houses at Knocknacarrow. He owned three properties in Dublin, all used for letting. He also owned three half-acre sites, one without planning and one with planning permission for a marina. He owned another site with two chalets under construction.

After learning that Geraldine Kennedy, Bruce Arnold, and Vincent Browne had been awarded damages for illegal tapping, I contacted the senior garda contact who had warned me that my phone was being tapped. I asked him if the information could be officially verified. He told me that he had met his contact in the Phoenix Park behind a tree, 200 yards from the roadway. He told me that this garda was involved in the tapping of phones by the government. It would be impossible for him to verify anything.

On a lighter note, when I told my family that our phone was tapped, my then 12-year-old daughter, Derina, picked up the 'phone every night for at least a week and said: "Goodnight Charlie"!

## GUESS WHO TAPPED THE GOVERNMENT ?

There were many audacious taps, official and unofficial, during the twelve years of Haughey's leadership. The most daring of all was the bugging of Government meetings – by the British Government!

The details were given to me by former Fianna Fáil TD and Minister Conor Lenihan, who heard the extraordinary story from his father, Brian.

During a period in 1988, Brian Lenihan, who was on his third term as Foreign Minister, was alerted to the taps by a close friend, the American Ambassador, Margaret Mary Heckler (nee O'Shaughnessy).

At a meeting over tea and cakes at the embassy, the ambassador dropped the bombshell: "Are you aware your Cabinet meetings are being bugged by the British?"

Subsequently, the Tánaiste called in communications expert Liam Brady, who told me that he swept the Cabinet room at that time. He discovered that the phone used by the Taoiseach was the problem. He said the British were tapping Haughey's personal communications phone.

Apparently, the Cabinet room had been regularly swept by the then Deputy Commissioner Joe Ainsworth who had responsibility for the widespread tapping – both legal and illegal – that went on at that time.

Strong representations were subsequently made to the British Prime Minister, Margaret Thatcher, about this "unfriendly and hostile act" – which was never made public.

Another celebrated bugging was the officially sanctioned tapping of journalists Bruce Arnold and Geraldine Kennedy, authorised by the then Minister for Justice, Sean Doherty, in 1982. They were later awarded €20,000 each by the State in 1987, while Arnold's wife, Mavis, received €10,000. The phone of journalist and broadcaster Vincent Browne was also tapped by successive governments, including the Haughey government. It has been reported that he received more than €90,000 in compensation.

Fianna Fáil politicians who were challenging the leadership of Haughey also believed their phones were illegally tapped. They included Ministers George Colley, Martin O'Donoghue, and Des O'Malley, as well as a former Lord Mayor of Dublin, Ben Briscoe, who placed a motion of no confidence in the Haughey leadership, and Wexford TD Hugh Byrne.

Haughey won the motion of no confidence in 1982, with 22 voting against. I often wondered would Haughey have survived had I given George Colley the explosive Doherty material, which was subsequently used by RTÉ in a documentary (see page 106).

Just before he was forced out of office in February, 1992, Haughey declared:

"I have always abhorred the principle of 'phone tapping, except where absolutely necessary to prevent serious crime or subversion by paramilitary organisations".

What about the time that he was tapping the 'phone of his Taoiseach, Jack Lynch in the late 1960's? Was that "absolutely necessary"?

At the time, Haughey was Minister for Finance. Post Office officials at the Merrion Exchange opposite Government buildings discovered a tap going from Haughey's office to the then Taoiseach, Jack Lynch. Every time the Taoiseach picked up his phone, Haughey could hear the conversation. The officials were Brian Killeen and his supervisor, Jim Dermody. An investigation was subsequently held by the Special Branch, but the result of it was never made public.

During Haughey's wilderness years, after he was dismissed from Government over his alleged involvement in the illegal importation of arms in 1970, there were regular taps on his home.

Special Branch, who were monitoring Haughey for many years and regularly tapping his phone, disclosed later to the Jack Lynch Government that Haughey had several meetings with leading members of the IRA – some at his mansion in Kinsealy.

But one of the most sensational of all was when Haughey was out of power. It has now been established that the Jack Lynch Government received a memorandum from Special Branch on his IRA activities.

The top-secret memo, which I have seen, came from the Special Branch and read:

"Mr Charles Haughey is still in touch with the Provisional IRA through John Kelly and Joe Cahill. He told them he was not in a position to do anything for them at present but that he hoped to be back in the Government in a few months' time and would press for a stronger line on the North. He told them that Special Branch, Dublin Castle, were still receiving information from inside the Republican movement but not as much as heretofore. He promises to pass on anything he hears on that aspect but to keep his name out of it".

That demonstrated that Haughey was prepared to act virtually as an informer or spy for the IRA: "He promises to pass on anything he hears but to keep his name out of it."

Former President Erskine Childers might have got it right when he said that Haughey should have been charged with treason during the Arms Crisis.

## FIANNA FÁIL IN AMERICA

When Haughey's successor, Albert Reynolds, became Taoiseach in February 1992, his top priority was to bring peace to Northern Ireland and steer the country's economic ship to even calmer waters.

The new Taoiseach took on board my suggestion when I sent him a memorandum on how the enormous goodwill that exists in America could be turned to Ireland's benefit. Almost fifty per cent of the chief executives of corporate America were of Irish extraction – an enormous resource never fully tapped or explored by an Irish Government. I suggested that the Irish semi-state bodies could research these top executives and find out who might be encouraged to invest in Ireland. Once the research was complete, these people should be contacted individually by the Taoiseach, touching sensitive egos. They would be particularly chuffed at being personally contacted by the Irish prime minister.

Reynolds took the suggestion on board, developing it even further. He established a high-profile economic committee whose job was to prepare a marketing policy for Ireland and act as a sounding board for ideas and policies. In the event of industrial problems, the Taoiseach could use the network of contacts to defuse any potential problems. This committee included Ireland's richest and most successful businessman, Tony O'Reilly, chairman and chief executive of H. J. Heinz and Independent Newspapers, Roy Disney, boss of the Walt Disney Company, former Coca Cola Chief Donald Keough, Fruit of the Loom boss John Holland, billionaire Chuck Feeney of Medallion Hotels, Bill Flynn of Mutual of America, Michael J. Roarty of Anheuser-Busch, Dan Rooney, owner of the Pittsburgh Steelers, General Electric boss John Welch, Peter Lynch of Fidelity Investments, Daniel Tully of Merrill Lynch and Co., Margaret Duffy of Arthur Anderson, Kerry-born Denis Kelleher of Wall Street Investor Services, Mary Maguire of the Chase Manhattan Bank, Brian Thompson of LUI International, John McGillicuddy of Chemical Banking Corporation, Daniel E. Gill of Bausch and Lomb in Rochester, Brian Burns of BF Enterprises, San Francisco, Boston businessmen Edmund Keely of Liberty Mutual Group, William Connell boss of the Connell Limited Partnership, Donald Brennan, boss of Morgan Stanley Banking Group, Andrew McKenna of Schwarz Paper Company, Illinois, and John Patrick Casey of KPMG Peat Marwick, New York.

Some years previously at a brief meeting, a similar suggestion was made to Haughey, but he took no action on it. In fairness, however, he was the first Irish Taoiseach to establish a party fund-raising committee in the States. In charge of the operation was his first cousin Barbara O'Neill, wife of the Cork-born New York restaurateur and publican, Terry O'Neill. The former director general of Bord Fáilte, Mayo-born Joe Malone was added. And Haughey sent Naoimh O'Connor, a daughter of his old friend and solicitor Pat O'Connor, to explore new ways of getting money to support Fianna Fáil activities. Initially, the group did well. The first $500-a-plate fund-raising event in the exclusive Racing Club in New York was a huge success. Haughey was piped into the room, and the evening was described as one of the most sophisticated ever held by Fianna Fáil. One of the guests picked up the bill for the evening. Some who attended were promised lucrative Government contracts in return for their support.

As the American committee was launched, the Taoiseach was deeply sceptical of the advice being given by the establishment within the Department of Foreign Affairs on the Northern Ireland issue. Haughey wanted the Irish Ambassador to Washington, Sean Donlon, moved. He believed that Donlon exceeded his brief in criticising the Irish National Caucus, headed by Sean McManus and Noraid. The success of Donlon in influencing the Carter administration and Congress had infuriated the Irish republican lobby, who had been effectively marginalised by his efforts. These republican groups looked to Haughey, to vindicate their cause by getting rid of the ambassador who had so effectively opposed their efforts. At the end of June in 1980, Sean Donlon was called back to Dublin and told that he was being moved to the post of Permanent Representative to the United Nations in New York. However, a major complication arose when the proposed move was opposed by the hugely influential "Four Horsemen" – Tipp O'Neill, Ted Kennedy, Pat Moynihan, and the then Governor of New York, Hugh Carey – who expressed their "deep hurt" at the proposed transfer. Haughey and his Minister for Foreign Affairs Brian Lenihan backed down. Haughey later said there was no foundation to the reports that Sean Donlon was to be moved. The Department of Foreign Affairs reported that the transfer of Donlon was "totally without foundation" and that another diplomat, Noel Dorr, was being appointed to the UN post.

The American fund-raising committee, appointed by Haughey, was called the Friends of Fianna Fáil. At a later stage, they organised a fund-raiser for the ailing Tánaiste, Brian Lenihan, who urgently needed a liver transplant in a Pittsburgh Hospital. That money was raised in a few days following a phone call from Haughey.

In the last few years of Haughey's leadership, the American dollar well was running dry, and the fund-raising committee was relatively inactive. Albert Reynolds totally revamped it, bringing in a well-respected senior Fianna Fáil figure, Eoin Ryan, to head it. The former Senator, who had influential business connections, had been on the party committee during the time of the leadership of Jack Lynch, but when Haughey took over Ryan did not like the way the finances were organised and so he resigned. Under the leadership of trustee Rich Howlin, a number of very successful golf classics were organised, and these reaped a rich harvest for the Soldiers of Destiny. The debt was reduced to a manageable £500,000 before Taoiseach Bertie Ahern took over from Albert Reynolds.

# ON THE FUNNY SIDE

## A PERSONAL ENCOUNTER

I vividly remember a controversial Dáil debate, led by the late Labour Leader, Frank Cluskey. He made serious allegations Haughey, who was then serving as Taoiseach, that he had made substantial money from a scam in the PMPA Insurance company.

I had excellent contacts in the PMPA, so I decided to investigate it. It turned out that there was absolutely no substance to the Cluskey allegations, so I wrote a lead story in my column "Backchat" for the *Sunday Independent*.

Walking down the corridor of the Dáil the following Tuesday, I bumped into the Taoiseach who was with a secretary.

"Did you write that story in the 'Backchat' column," he inquired.

"Yes I did," I replied.

He put out his hand to shake mine and said: "Thanks."

I answered: "You know me well enough to know if it was true, I would have written that story."

He replied: "I have no problem with that."

As he was walking away, I could not resist asking him: "Would you recommend Le Coq Hardi for a meal?"

He looked back at me with a nasty scowl.

## MISTAKEN IDENTITY

Charlie Haughey's wry comment on journalists, "I hate those creeping little shits", reminds me of my first meeting with him in 1981.

I was sent by the *Sunday Independent* to do a colour story on Haughey who was on the campaign trail in Co. Kerry. In the company of one of Charlie's minders, Eoin Patton, I flew to Farranfore Airport. From there, I was chauffeur-driven to Kenmare, where the Taoiseach was electioneering in typical rambunctious style with outgoing Deputy John O'Leary from Killarney and a rising young star from Cahirciveen, solicitor and later Minister for Justice John O'Donoghue.

I was eagerly looking forward to that first meeting, as I had read that Charlie was brilliant, erudite, eloquent and had taken first place in Ireland in his primary certificate, had won first-class honours in all his subjects in UCD, and had qualified as a chartered accountant and a barrister. He was also an expert on Irish and French history, fluent in both languages, and a connoisseur on French wines.

During our brief meeting, I had hoped he would share some nuggets of wisdom.

In the back of a helicopter for three hours with his then press secretary, Frank Dunlop, I was seated only a couple of feet from this wonderful man of letters, this walking genius.

All he said to me during that time was four words: "Close that fucking door!"

Charlie thought I was a member of his security!

## UNEASY RELATIONS WITH THE MEDIA

Haughey's uneasy relations with the media go way back, almost to the start of his political career in the late fifties. One of the first controversies he became involved in concerned the sale of his home in Raheny for €204, 000 – a figure worth more than ten times as much in to-day's money. On his case in the election of 1969 was the Labour candidate Dr. Conor Cruise O'Brien. He pointed out that the value of the house and forty acres of land had rocketed from around €50,000 because he had been granted planning permission for house building, though the land was situated in a green belt. Questions were asked if Haughey had inside knowledge of what was happening.

Pat Cashman, a photographer from *The Irish Press* was sent to get a picture of the house. Maureen Haughey answered the door but closed it without saying anything when Cashman explained why he had come. He decided to take pictures of the house anyway and was snapping away merrily when a Mercedes car swept into the driveway. Haughey got out and began to harangue him. Newspaper photographers are rough diamonds, and Pat Cashman is a veteran of many newsrooms. But he recalled: "I was subjected to a torrent of foul-mouthed abuse of a kind I've never heard before or since."

Haughey's ferocious tongue was one of his most notable characteristics. But it was rarely employed against the media. His own press officers were a different matter. Political Correspondents recall seeing Haughey abusing Frank Dunlop, government press secretary, at an EU presidency meeting, over some perceived failure. Dunlop interrupted him: "If you keep going on like that, I'll walk away." Haughey continued his tirade, so Dunlop walked away with the Taoiseach shouting after him: "Don't you fucking walk away from me." In a roundabout apology, the following day, Haughey rang Dunlop's wife who was expecting a baby at the time, to enquire how she was getting on and to tell her everything was going well at the EU meeting.

Everyone agrees that Haughey's great gift was to keep people guessing, so that they were never sure what he would do next. "He always seemed to have an innate sense of people's weaknesses," says one insider. "He always knew where and when to put on the pressure. But if he was ultimately resisted, he would go at it a different way. He had endless ways of putting people under stress." In his youth, according to classmates, he learnt lines of poetry in Latin and Irish as well as English. He would quote these at appropriate moments to undermine civil servants and politicians or journalists, knowing that very few would have enough education to respond in kind.

Haughey did not cultivate journalists in quite the same way as he did select politicians, business, and artistic people. A few hacks were permitted into the inner sanctum of Kinsealy for legendary late-night drinking sessions. But it was a precarious privilege, for they were always in dread of having their licence unceremoniously terminated at the whim of their host.

*His master's voice: P. J. Mara.*

With journalists outside the charmed circle, he had to be more circumspect. One of these was Bruce Arnold of the Irish Independent. Arnold had been trying to get an interview with Haughey for several weeks. He made his way into Government Buildings and as Haughey was walking down the corridor to his office, Arnold suddenly appeared from a side door and started asking questions. Haughey was perfectly polite: "I haven't got time now. Make an appointment." But when the journalist had been ushered away, Haughey turned furiously on his officials: "Don't ever let him in here again," he roared. Arnold never got the appointment.

Haughey was funny about interviews. There were things he did not want to discuss. The government press secretary from 1987, the legendary P. J. Mara made an uncharacteristic slip during an official visit to Australia. Briefing journalists about what would happen and what questions they could ask, Mara quipped: "And no oul' arms trial shite!." Most of the Australian journalists had never heard of the 1970 trial when Haughey was charged and acquitted of illegally importing arms for use in Northern Ireland. But once alerted, they were very interested!

On the rare occasions when he did give interviews, journalists came to know some of Haughey's psychological tricks to gain the high ground. This usually consisted of saying at the last moment that he had decided not to do the interview, or even that he did not know anything about the journalist involved. The idea may have been that by the time the interview started, the desperate reporter would be glad to get anything from "the Squire".

On one occasion he was interviewed by the US network ABC. The crew was willing to submit written questions, which was perfect for Haughey, who was conscious that the network had a huge audience in the US. But when the crew arrived for their morning appointment, Haughey refused to open his office door and responded to requests with "Fuck off, go away."

Eventually an official discovered that the problem was not stage fright, but a raging hangover from a night spent consuming copious quantities of vintage claret. Haughey was slumped over his desk, holding the list of questions. "I can't do it" he muttered. "Tell them to go away."

The civil servant knew the solution. He quickly ordered Orange juice and black coffee. In due course, Haughey recovered sufficiently to answer the questions. The German crew, who were operating for ABC were very puzzled by the mysterious goings on – but left reasonably happy with the result.

As the telephone tapping affair in 1982 showed, Haughey was as obsessed with media coverage of himself and his administration as any other politician. But his suspicions of journalists in general meant he was less active about briefing and even leaking to selected journalists in the way that most politicians do.

Sometimes, through his mistress, Terry Keane, when she was working for the Sunday Independent, he did leak stories about the love life of several members of his Government colleagues. And when the Pope arrived in September 1979, there was a huge controversy about a story involving the late President Paddy Hillery. Political correspondents were called before their editors to brief them how to handle the story. Hillery blamed Haughey for leaking the story, which alleged he had an affair with a secretary in Brussels while he was an EU Commissioner.

A Taoiseach's main contacts with the press are with its political correspondents covering Leinster House. Haughey always kept his distance from them, but those who were in favour were invited to his office for background briefings occasionally. Fianna Fáil's Christmas parties for the press were legendary for their liquid hospitality. The political correspondents always received a present of a bottle of spirits – Tullamore Dew, Redbreast, Scotch or even Bushmills – from Haughey personally.

One correspondent, who may have been in disfavour at the time, went to Haughey's office to collect his present. Haughey did not give it to him but gradually kept pushing it across the desk, a little at a time, as they were talking. Eventually the confused hack had to move quickly to catch the bottle before it fell to the floor! He left in a sweat, clutching his hard-won present.

## A THATCHER MOMENT

Haughey's attention to detail was legendary. For the European Summit in Dublin in 1990 he dispatched to Brussels his head of protocol at Dublin Castle, Vincent Cullen, to research how the Belgians were handling "Yer wan" – as he referred to Thatcher.

Before he left, he received a blunt message from Haughey: "I want ours to be fucking better! Keep your eyes open and have a look around and go up and check what "yer wan is getting". Vincent did his job thoroughly. He peered into her bedroom, checked out her bathroom and discovered that she had especially installed all sorts of exotic perfumes, soaps, towels and toiletries.

Six months later, it was Ireland's turn to host the European summit at Dublin Castle. Haughey met Cullen and said: "I hope you will have the place looking well for 'yer wan' to-morrow". He

*Haughey greets "Yer wan".*

instructed him to put everything Irish in the room. Cullen bought all his toiletries in Arnott's.

As usual, Haughey inspected all the rooms at Dublin Castle before Thatcher arrived. He was accompanied by his press secretary, P. J. Mara, who immediately sampled the Thatcher bed and joked irreverently: "This will do the oul' bitch". Haughey peeped into the bathroom and shouted at Vincent: "This is a bit much!". He was looking at the well-known Irish cologne – Man of Aran, by Vincent!

Thatcher was obviously pleased with the Irish perfumes and toiletries. When staff arrived to clean up the rooms after the summit was over, the toiletries were all cleared from her bathroom!

Earlier, the Taoiseach was informed by one of his officials that the Thatcher helicopter was approaching Dublin Castle. A couple of moments later, the same official announced: "She has arrived now, Taoiseach".

Haughey walked out on the bridge to meet her. The wind from the motor blades blew his hair all over the place. He went back inside the door, wet his fingers and with difficulty managed to pat his hair down. An official said to the Taoiseach: "She is on the bottom step now". Haughey stepped out again and the wind stood his hair up again. He turned to his bemused officials: "Ah fuck it, let her come to me."

## HAUGHEY'S VIEW OF GANGSTERS

The former Minister for the Environment, Ray Burke, asked Charlie Haughey to open a new lounge in his constituency in Swords, north Dublin.

Over cocktails, the Taoiseach pointed to a picture of actor Edward G. Robinson, who played in a lot of gangster films: "I see you're remembered here," he said.

Burke countered: "Yes, but you're in the next lounge."

They both walked to the next room to see a picture of actor Robert de Niro in one of his most famous roles – as gangster Al Capone!

## NUCLEAR MISSILES IN WICKLOW

Back in Dublin in early 1980 after an important meeting in Washington, the Tánaiste and Foreign Minister Brian Lenihan could not contain himself. In a Dublin pub early in the morning he disclosed to a close friend one of the most bizarre tales of the entire Haughey era.

At the time Ireland was heavily in debt, and the International Monetary Fund had made overtones to the Government to take corrective measures.

In a celebrated television broadcast, the new Taoiseach, Charles Haughey, had told the nation that we were living way beyond our means and urged us to tighten our belts. (He never told us that he was then spending €26,000 per month, buying expensive presents and wining and dining his mistress, Terry Keane).

This was the time when the whole international scene had been thrown into turmoil by the invasion of Afghanistan by the Russians, and the Americans were worried that this was the beginning of a new push by the Soviets to extend their sphere of influence around the world.

In the pub, Lenihan told his friend that the officials in the Washington administration had come up with a solution to our dire financial problems. They would clear the debt – provided we would agree to an unusual quid pro quo.

Swearing his friend to secrecy, he revealed that the Americans wanted the Irish Government to provide a suitable site to house a nuclear arsenal in Ireland. They suggested that an ideal location was the hydroelectric power station at Turlough Hill, about forty miles from Dublin. The ESB had excavated a huge area of rock under the mountain and ran a shaft up the centre to enable turbines to be driven by water tumbling from the mountaintop. The Americans proposed to install the nuclear arsenal covertly beside the generators under the mountain.

In the end, the proposal came to naught because the Americans had second thoughts and Haughey dismissed it out of hand, saying that having American missiles under an Irish mountain would totally compromise the country's neutrality!

## NEW WINE INTO OLD

At one point about ten men were working on Haughey's island home at Inishvickillane in Co. Kerry. The men were a thirsty lot and when they did their stint, they would bring out five or six barrels of Guinness. The leader of the group, Dan Brick, was about to sail to the mainland at the weekend when the weather broke.

In the house, they discovered bottles of wine, not knowing they were vintage. As the storm continued to blow for a couple of days, they polished them off. When they eventually returned to the mainland they headed straight to Garvey's supermarket in Dingle, where they bought a quantity of red wine for just £1.50 a bottle. After returning to the island, they poured the new wine back into the bottles that had held the vintage wine and placed the old corks back.

The following summer Haughey returned to his cellar with a person he was eager to impress. Proudly, he showed him a bottle of

POLITICAL BETRAYAL

*Islandman: about to start the Dingle Regatta on one of his visits to Inishvickillane.*

his "vintage" wine and, with the room at the right temperature, uncorked it. He asked his guest to sample it first. The VIP did not want to insult his host, so he said it was "perfect".

Then Haughey took a sip, and immediately spat it out. It tasted like vinegar. He tasted some of the other bottles. Again, the taste was bitter. He was mystified for almost a year until he met Dan Brick on the island.

Innocently, Dan told Haughey how they had run out of drink during a storm the previous year, so they drank the wine in the old bottles. Sensing that there was something seriously wrong by the stunned look on Haughey's face, Dan added: "But we replaced it all."

Haughey's reaction? According to close friends, he nearly fell off his chair laughing, and it became a story he liked to tell often!

## THE MEDJUGORJE TOUCH

One of Haughey's most loyal supporters down through the years was former Senator and Westmeath hotelier Donie Cassidy.

Elected to the Labour panel of the Seanad for twenty years in succession (from 1982 to 2002), he had to be an outstanding

*Talking to local politician Jackie Healy-Rae on a visit to south Kerry.*

canvasser. Unlike a number of politicians who lectured to their electorate – county councillors, TDs, and Senators – Donie did thorough research on every candidate and listened to any helpful detail about the councillor he was canvassing.

Why was he so successful as a poll topper? This vignette might explain his popularity.

Driving up a boreen to meet a councillor in North Cork, he brought along the local Fianna Fáil TD, Larry Kelly.

"Give me some background on this councillor", pleaded Donie.

"Oh, he's very big into Medjugorje" replied Larry.

"Medjugorje", exclaimed Cassidy.

Donie searched deep in his pocket and produced a medal from the little village in Yugoslavia where six teenage girls saw a vision of the Blessed Virgin in 1981.

Donie and Larry Kelly were greeted by the local councillor, called Mick, and his wife and teenage children, who were given tapes of the midlands group, Foster and Allen.

Six weeks after the election, where Donie again topped the poll, Larry Kelly met the councillor at a local function.

"What way did you vote in that last Senate election", asked Larry.

Mick replied: "I was very confused. They were coming at me from every angle. Professors, lawyers, doctors…but I'll tell you one thing…I gave the number one to the fellow from Medjugorje!"

## A SACKING MATTER

Finally, I would like to share with you a story that has been re-told down the years as part of Limerick journalistic lore.

The then editor and proprietor of the *Limerick Weekly Echo*, the late Tommy Morris, was in his office, dictating a letter to his secretary. He heard noise coming next door from the newsroom. He asked his secretary what was the noise.

"A typewriter," she answered.

His next question: "Who is typing?"

"Christy Bannon."

He shouted: "Bannon! Send him in here!"

Christy Bannon, a court and general reporter who also wrote a weekly column, stood tall before his boss.

Morris: "Didn't I fire you last Friday?"

"You did, Tommy."

"Did you get my letter confirming you were fired?"

"Yes, Tommy."

"Did you get the solicitor's letter confirming my letter?"

"I did, Tommy."

"Well, what do you have to say?"

"Tommy, this ball-hopping will have to stop!"

For the remainder of his long career, Christy Bannon was never sacked again.

# THE HAUGHEY LEGACY: THE GOOD, THE BAD, AND THE UGLY

## HIS GREATEST SERVICE

The restoration of the government finances after 1987 was an outstanding achievement for Haughey and for his then Minister for Finance, Ray McSharry. But Haughey's greatest service to the nation was the introduction of the International Financial Services Centre.

The importance of the IFSC to the Irish economy is indisputable. In 2021, total employment stands at over 44,000 with 10,000 people employed outside Dublin. More than €1 billion is paid in corporate taxes each year, with a further €1 billion going to the Exchequer in payroll taxes. The average salary of each worker is €60,000 a year. It has become one of the leading hedge fund service centres in Europe. Many of the world's most important financial institutions have a presence there.

Fourteen of the top fifteen global lessors are now based in Ireland, with more than €4 trillion in fund assets, seventeen of the top twenty global banks, and eleven of the top fifteen insurance companies worldwide. The IFSC is also host to half of the world's top fifty banks and to half of the top twenty insurance companies.

There have been dramatic changes in the composition of the international financial services industry with a loss in banking jobs but gains in fund administration, insurance, aircraft leasing, and payments. Employment growth has been driven by technology focused roles and has reflected Ireland's ability to combine financial services and ICT strengths. IFSC companies now account for about thirty-eight per cent of all financial services corporation tax revenues.

The IFSC was established with EU approval by the Haughey-led government in 1987. The concept originally came from international financier Dermot Desmond, who was a strong proponent of the idea of building a financial centre on Dublin's derelict docklands and promoting it with generous tax rates. Garret FitzGerald as Taoiseach did not move on the plan because he worried how the tax incentives could be confined to foreign institutions. He thought the IFSC could

*The IFSC: a brainchild of Dermot Desmond's put into effect by Haughey.*

not be completely ring-fenced for foreigners. Haughey, however, had no qualms about that and when he took over as Taoiseach ordered a team of civil servants to implement the plan. He exerted the full force of his powers as the "Boss" to get the project moving in quick time. It offered the prospect of substantial immediate construction jobs and the long-term revitalisation of rundown areas.

Dermot Desmond was the most remarkable of Haughey's business friends and associates. He was also different from the others, both in terms of the relationship and the kind of businessman he is. The others tended to be part of Haughey's circle and were accountants, like Des Traynor, or property developers, like John Byrne. Desmond seems genuinely to have admired Haughey's abilities, and particularly his determination to get things done.

Talent and the ability to get things done, are certainly Desmond hallmarks. As the son of a customs officer (who ironically was stationed at Dublin Airport during the attempt to import arms for which Haughey later stood trial and was acquitted), Desmond did

*Desmond admired Haughey's ability to get things done.*
PHOTOGRAPH: MATT KAVANAGH, *THE IRISH TIMES*

not have any automatic entrée into the world of finance. However, after a spell working with the World Bank, he decided that was exactly where he was going to work. He did not like the fact that stockbroking in Dublin was dominated by a handful of firms, most of them associated with old Protestant money.

He founded National City Brokers (NCB) as a money-broker – someone that essentially shaves fractions off the cost of money for clients. This was a business where skill and ingenuity were more important than the personal connections that dominated conventional stockbroking.

NCB was sufficiently successful to move on into share and bond dealing and to rank eventually as one of the "Big Four" firms with Davys, Riada, and Goodbodys. It was a remarkable achievement to come from nowhere in a business where many of the firms were founded in the nineteenth century.

Along the way, he showed much of the original vision that has characterised most of his investment decisions. He was not content just to have NCB buy the fancy computer equipment central to modern financial dealing. He spun off a successful company that designed software for the industry. He was also an early investor in Irish cream liqueurs – one of the great marketing success stories of modern times.

Among the initial incentives for companies locating in the docklands zone were a ten per cent rate of corporation tax; exemption from rates for ten years; double rent allowances against trading income for the first ten years; 100 per cent capital allowance; no stamp duty; and no exchange controls for dealing in foreign currencies to overseas clients; and zero VAT on services from the centre.

When Haughey gave an interview in 1988 to Euromoney, a global finance magazine, Dermot Desmond helped to write Haughey's IFSC sales pitch. The close collaboration between Haughey and Desmond in marketing the new centre is disclosed in Department of the Taoiseach documents released under the thirty-year rule.

Haughey would not do a face-to-face interview but agreed to respond to questions put in writing by the magazine. The records contain drafts of his detailed answers, including a last draft. A note in handwriting states: "Final version cleared but to include Dermot Desmond's comments as considered suitable."

Desmond's hand-written amendments included references to a network of double taxation agreements, an observation that Ireland's regulatory standards were the "very highest", and a reference to Ireland's focus on technology-related financial services.

Desmond wrote: "We believe that our excellent communications facilities and computer literate workforce can give us a stronger competitive edge in this area. I believe that Ireland can become a significant springboard for US and Japanese institutions building a presence in EEC financial markets."

In 2019, the Government developed a revised strategy for the growth of the IFSC, which it hoped would deliver 5,000 new jobs between 2020 and 2025. This, in fact, is half the level of job creation of previous IFS strategies and reflects the Government's assessment that artificial intelligence technology and increased automation in financial services could lead to a reduction in the number of jobs in certain areas of the industry.

The focus of the new strategy is to ensure that jobs located here are "high quality and well paid", while also supporting the location of a significant number of jobs outside Dublin.

The new strategy is designed to ensure Ireland retains its leadership role in IFS, in the face of increasing competition from other EU member states and the likes of Singapore, Hong Kong, and Israel.

## INEXPENSIVE GESTURES

While the IFSC is a remarkable achievement, Haughey's classic, low-cost gestures were sprinkled throughout his career.

The granting of tax-free status to creative artists was a low-cost imaginative gesture. The measure persuaded some wealthy foreign writers and filmmakers to live in Ireland. It also fitted nicely with Haughey's image of himself as a Renaissance-style patron of the arts. He set up the Aosdána scheme in 1982, a group of 250 self-chosen artists, some of whom who are entitled to grants from the State.

He also appreciated the value of Dublin's historic buildings and the need to preserve them. The restoration of the Royal Hospital at Kilmainham and the sale of the Georgian houses in Merrion Street for restoration as part of the luxury Merrion Hotel are down to him. So is the refurbishment of Government Buildings and its use for the purpose which it is believed the British secretly intended it when it was built during the agitation for Home Rule.

Haughey believed in the power of inexpensive but imaginative gestures. The most effective was probably the introduction of free travel on public transport and free TV licenses for old-age pensioners when he was Minister for Finance in 1967.

But there is a question mark now over whether it was Haughey who thought about the free travel concept. Sources close to the great man disclosed that the free travel suggestion came from his wife, Maureen.

## DEV'S FOREBODING

Did the late President de Valera have a foreboding about Haughey in his final years in the Áras? It seems he did.

We have established that in private conversations with the then Taoiseach, Jack Lynch, and some of his Cabinet in 1970 he issued a profound warning about Haughey. These private meetings were held in the Áras, as the Arms Crisis exploded on the nation.

The members of Cabinet were then told by the 88-year-old that Haughey, who had been charged with smuggling illegal arms into the country, would, if unchecked, inflict great damage to the party and to the country.

He also told some members of the then Cabinet that because of Haughey, divisions and bitterness would last within Fianna Fáil for years. Later events revealed the accuracy of Dev's warning. Over many decades, Haughey's poisonous effect on the internal affairs of Fianna Fáil and on democracy in general was disclosed.

Even Sean Lemass, Haughey's father-in-law, had his reservations. Before Lemass announced his retirement as Taoiseach in 1966, he sent a message to one of the contenders, George Colley, to return from the States. "Your return should not be delayed" was his message. Colley was subsequently beaten by Jack Lynch in the election stakes.

In the mid-1950s Lemass and President Sean T. O'Kelly were having lunch in Roundwood, Co. WIcklow. Casually, Sean T mentioned: "I see where the young buck Haughey is courting your daughter, Maureen. Who knows, they might end up marrying."

Lemass was not amused, responding curtly: "Over my dead body!"

More than ten years later, a friend was chatting with Lemass in

THE HAUGHEY LEGACY

Haughey's house, away from the revelry going on outside in the garden. The friend commented on the superb antiques, including the furniture, paintings, and silver in the spacious hallway. He joked that with that crowd outside, the family better keep an eye on the antiques.

Lemass let his eyes sweep around the walls at the magnificent antiques. "Ah yes" he said, "but where did all the money come from to buy the antiques!"

Frank Aiken, War of Independence veteran and former Minister for Foreign Affairs, was so strongly opposed to Haughey after the Arms Crisis that he refused to stand for re-election in 1973. He made it clear to Jack Lynch that his reason was Haughey's continued support from the leadership.

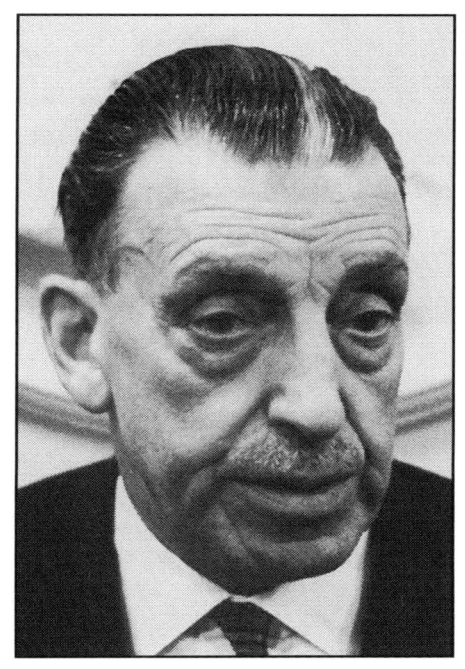

*Sean Lemass had misgivings about his son-in-law.*

President Erskine Childers had similar views on Haughey, calling his actions leading to the Arms Crisis as "treason". During his presidential election, he refused to canvass in Haughey's constituency of Dublin North-Central. When it was pointed out that he would potentially lose thousands of votes, he replied: "I would rather die than be photographed beside him."

Sean MacEntee, a long-standing senior member of Fianna Fáil TD who had held several ministerial posts, had a visit from Haughey when he was nearing the end of his days in 1984. Haughey had a photographer with him. But the visit ended when MacEntee

159

*Haughey and Brian Lenihan with Erskine Childers at a party Ardfheis. Childers later said, "I would rather die than be photographed beside him."*

emphatically refused to be photographed with Haughey.

### THE LENIHAN FUND

What undoubtedly did the most damage to Haughey's reputation was his treatment of Brian Lenihan, after he was asked to organise a fund-raising venture for his friend who urgently needed a liver transplant at an American hospital. The Moriarty Tribunal, which spent thirteen years investigating Haughey, found that he "personally misappropriated" a large amount of the funds raised in the US for the man he described as his "closest political friend".

In blunt terms, the tribunal chairman said that it gave him no satisfaction to find that Haughey deliberately encouraged fund-raising on a scale beyond what was needed and that he used the surplus money for himself.

A total of €336,000 was raised for the operation but just €88,000 was actually required. This allowed Haughey to misappropriate almost €250,000. And it was done in a clever fashion, as the money was lodged to the leader's account, so that nobody within Fianna

Fáil would question him.

The tribunal report was scathing on Haughey, stating it was "reprehensible" of him to try to blame others.

## HAUGHEY'S GENEROSITY TO CONSTITUENTS

Haughey's generosity was well known in his sprawling constituency of Dublin North Central, made up mostly of a working-class population with pockets of unemployment as bad as could be found anywhere in the country. For any death or accident among his constituents, the family concerned received a bouquet of flowers. One family in Donnycarney had all their furniture and carpets destroyed in a fire; Haughey instructed his secretary, Catherine, to have the house re-furnished.

He was particularly generous at Christmas time. The manager of a local supermarket was asked by him to hand out fifty hampers to the neediest. Haughey paid the bill and told the manager not to mention his name in connection with the gift.

While canvassing during an election campaign, he noticed that an old woman living alone needed her fireplace fixed. The fireplace was repaired and next day she got a delivery of a ton of coal. In another case, Haughey sent a lawyer to a woman with a legal problem and again paid the bill. When he attended the funeral in Tipperary of the father of his Northern Ireland advisor, Dr Martin Mansergh, a youngster knocked at the window of his State car to say hello. Haughey rolled down the window, smiled, and handed the boy a €5 note.

## A CULTURE OF CORRUPTION

Finally, while Haughey has some outstanding achievements, it seems we are equivocal about his misdeeds – because we are not sure if he did anything all that wrong.

The facts are that according to the Moriarty Tribunal he trousered

CARTOON BY ANNE WOODFULL

millions while in office. They put a figure of €45 million in to-day's money. We now know it is much more than that – close to €70 million.

Haughey contaminated politics, and we must always remember that it is a crime to enrich yourself while serving the public. He brought greed to the pinnacle of our politics, was a kept man – bought and paid for by Ireland's most successful businessmen.

Unfortunately, during the Haughey years the culture of corruption operated from the top and percolated through the whole system, contaminating the body politic. Haughey had betrayed the public trust and reaped a huge dividend for his efforts for himself throughout his career.

While the media can be faulted for not laying a glove on him during his leadership years, it took two tribunals more than twelve years to pinpoint the extent of his corruption during his time in politics. His words to the Dáil during the Arms Crisis of 1970 now appear to be brim-full of hypocrisy. He said then: "Since becoming a Minister I have endeavoured to the best of my ability to serve my country, Dáil Éireann and the Government. I have never at any time acted in breach of the trust reposed in me."

As a Minister and later Taoiseach, it was incumbent on him to set an example and uphold the highest standards of propriety. He failed miserably to do that. Also he made one re-occurring mistake throughout his long career. This was particularly true in the disgraceful way he pocketed the Brian Lenihan liver transplant money. He thought he was untouchable. Thankfully, the Moriarty Tribunal had other ideas.

# INDEX

# INDEX

## A

Abdullah, Crown Prince 90
Adams, Gerry 46, 47, 48, 53
Ainsworth, Joe 88, 111
Alton, Professor Brian 14
Andreotti, Giulio 92
Arnold, Bruce 86, 88, 108, 110, 111, 142
Arnold, Mavis 111

## B

Bannon, Christy 150
Barbour, Captain Ollie 79, 80
Barrett, Sylvester 79
Berry, Peter 11, 12, 13, 33, 34, 35, 38, 40, 41, 68
Blaney, Neil 33, 35, 36, 37, 38, 39
Boland, Kevin 39, 42, 43, 78, 129, 132
Boorman, John 24
Bowler, Gillian 23
Brady, Liam 111
Brennan, Donald 114
Brennan, Ned 69
Brennan, Seamus 3, 67, 69, 70, 114
Brick, Dan 147, 148
Briscoe, Ben 66, 108, 111
Browne, Vincent 42, 43, 110, 111
Bulger, James 'Whitey' 52
Burke, Ray 96, 129, 130, 146
Burns, Brian 114

Bush, George 92
Butler, Catherine 79, 93, 96, 161
Byrne, Hugh 111
Byrne, John 154

## C

Cahill, Joe 44, 51, 52, 112
Campbell-Sharpe, Noelle 27
Capone, Al 146
Carey, Hugh 115
Carpenter, Carl 20
Carpenter, Holly 20
Carpenter, Jane 19, 20
Carty, Michael 41
Casey, John Patrick 114
Cashman, Pat 140, 141
Cassells, Peter 94
Cassidy, Donie 148
Childers, President Erskine 41, 113, 159, 160
Clinton, President Bill 53
Cluskey, Frank 139
Cole, Dermot 130
Colleary, Padraig 132
Colley, George 52, 77, 85, 101, 102, 108, 111, 124, 128, 158
Collins. Gerry 77, 96
Connell, William 114
Cosgrave, Liam 33, 35, 37, 38
Coughlan, Clem 66
Cox, Pat 106

Cronin, Tony 93
Cullen, Vincent 144, 145

## D

Day-Lewis, Daniel 24
Denieffe, Michael 104, 107
de Niro, Robert 146
Dermody, Jim 51, 112
Desmond, Dermot 127, 153, 154, 155, 156
de Valera, Eamon 34, 39, 65, 68, 95, 158
de Valera, Sile 68
Devine, John 105
Dillon, James 62, 64
Disney, Roy 114
Doherty, Maura 87
Doherty, Sean 6, 7, 68, 86, 87, 88, 90, 101, 102, 103, 104, 107, 108, 109, 110, 111
Donlon, Sean 115
Donnellan, Sean 71
Donnelly, Jimmy 19
Doolan, Professor Jim 77, 78
Dorr, Noel 115
Doyle, P.V. 24
Duffy, Margaret 114
Dully, Martin 28
Dunlop, Frank 26, 67, 140, 141
Dunne, Ben 66, 98, 99, 100, 108, 111, 124, 131, 132, 133, 134, 135

## F

Fallon, Sean 85
Fanning, Aengus 107
Farrell, Pat 95
Feeney, Chuck 114
Ferris, Martin 53, 64
Finn, Vincent 76
FitzGerald, Dr Garret 38, 77, 78, 104, 153
Fitzgerald, Liam 68, 69
Fleming, John 66
Flynn, Bill 114
Flynn, Padraig 6, 68, 85
Ford, Chris 99
Forsyth, Frederick 53, 54
Foxe, Tom 68
Foy, Eileen 93
Fustok, Mahmoud 89, 90, 135

## G

Gaddafi, Colonel Mu'ammar 52, 87
Geoghegan-Quinn, Maire 68, 129, 130
Gibbons, Jim 36, 38, 39, 40, 43, 52, 77
Gilchrist, Sir Andrew 49
Gill, Daniel E. 114
Goodman, Larry 127
Goulding, Cathal 44, 49
Guilfoyle, Christy 15, 16

# H

Hand, Michael 7, 102, 103, 104, 105, 106, 107, 109
Hanley, Peter 86
Harris, Pino 119, 120
Haughey, Charles
    alleged horsefall incident 11-16; taste for expensive shrts 24-25; affair with Terry Keane 17-30; the Arms Crisis 33-43; Northern Ireland peace moves 44-48; IRA spy allegation 48-54; secret courts 59-65; his fight for political survival 65-72; clash with Liam Lawlor 73-76; threats to garda and army officer 78-80; loss of power 85-91; final days as Taoiseach 91-97; the Carysfort deal 119-121; tangled personal finances 121-127; passport investment scheme 128-130; appearing before the McCracken and Moriarty Tribunals 131-136; relations with the media 140-144; setting up the IFSC 153-157; views of de Valera and Lemass on 158-161; generosity to constituents 161; handling of the Lenihan fund 160-161

Haughey, Ciaran 28, 92, 96, 121, 126
Haughey, Conor 96, 110, 121, 126, 140
Haughey, Eimear 92, 96, 121, 126
Haughey, Maureen 14, 30, 90, 94, 96, 140, 158
Haughey, Sean 69, 96, 126
Hawke, Bob 92
Hayes, Joe 105
Healy, John 61, 149
Healy-Rae, Jackie 149
Heaney, Michael 106
Heaney, Seamus 23
Heckler, Mary 110
Hederman, Dr Billy 14
Hillery, President Patrick 79, 80, 143, 144
Hogan, Lieutenant-General Louis 80
Holland, John 114
Howard, Catherine 21
Howard, John 21
Howlin, Richard 116
Hume, John 46, 47, 53, 93, 94
Hussey, Gemma 76, 77

# J

Jones, Gerry 27

# K

Keane, Chief Justice Ronan 19, 27

Keane, John B. 28
Keane, Terry 3, 6, 7, 17, 18, 19, 20, 21, 23, 25, 28, 30, 54, 96, 121, 126, 143, 146
Keely, Edmund 114
Kelleher, Denis 114
Kelly, Captain James 38, 39
Kelly, John 39, 43, 44, 51, 112
Kelly, Larry 149, 150
Kemmy, Jim 78
Kennedy, Geraldine 86, 88, 92, 108, 110, 111, 115
Kennedy, Ted 92, 115
Kenny, Patrick 129
Keogh, Dermot 6, 13
Keogh, Supt. Eamonn 6
Keough, Donald 114
Khan, Frank 106
Killeen, Brian 49, 112

## L

Lawlor, Liam 73, 74, 75, 76
Legge, Hector 33
Lemass, Sean 62, 95, 158, 159
Lenihan, Ann 125
Lenihan, Brian 26, 41, 70, 71, 79, 86, 87, 96, 110, 115, 124, 125, 135, 146, 160
Lenihan, Conor 110
Leyden, Terry 108
Loftus, Sean Dublin Bay 78

Lowry, Michael 131
Luykx, Albert 39
Lydon, Don 72
Lynch, Jack 11, 13, 15, 16, 28, 33, 34, 35, 38, 39, 41, 43, 44, 49, 51, 52, 67, 77, 95, 112, 114, 116, 124, 158, 159
Lynch, Peter 114

## M

MacEntee, Sean 159
Maguire, Mary 114
Mahfouz, Sheikh Khalid bin 128, 129
Major, John 47
Malone, Joe 114
Mansergh, Dr Martin 45, 47, 93, 161
Mara, P. J. 19, 20, 28, 96, 142, 145
Martin, Claire 28
Martin, Professor Gus 28
Masterson, Dr Paddy 119, 120
McAnally, Ray 28
McCracken, Mr Justice 131, 133
McCreevy, Charlie 85, 102
McCullough, Denis 132
McGillicuddy, John 114
McGonigal, Eoin 133
McKenna, Andrew 114
McMahon, Private Jim 14
McManus, Sean 115
McSharry, Ray 153
Mitchell, Gay 129, 130

# INDEX

Mitterrand, President François 17, 71, 127, 128
Moore, Kevin 106
Morgan, Donagh 93, 96, 114
Morris, Tommy 150
Mulholland, Joe 106
Mullan, Des 14
Mulrooney, Brian 92
Murphy, Ned 33, 43
Murphy, Paul 5, 33, 43, 103
Murphy, Supt. M.R. 5
Murray, Frank 121

## N

Nally, Derek 94, 101, 104, 105
Nally, Dermot 94
Noonan, Michael 86

## O

O'Brien, Bobby 94
O'Brien, Conor Cruise 140
O'Brien, Fergus 22, 69, 94
O'Brien, Sean 69
Ó Caoimh, Justice Aindrias 39
O'Connell, Dr John 45, 59, 89, 90, 91, 103, 122, 123
O'Coonor, Derina 110
O'Connor, Kevin 30
O'Connor, Naoimh 114
O'Connor, Patrick 14, 96, 114

O'Donoghue, John 139
O'Donoghue, Martin 85, 102, 108, 111
Ó hAnracháin, Pádraig 26, 67
Ó hUiginn, Pádraig 94
O'Kelly, Sean T. 158
O'Leary, Dermot 89, 90, 139
O'Leary, John 139
O'Mahony, Michael 103
O'Malley, Daragh 19, 20, 136
O'Malley, Des 3, 11, 12, 13, 19, 20, 39, 40, 41, 60, 61, 64, 66, 73, 75, 85, 102, 105, 106, 108, 111
O'Malley, Donogh 13, 19, 20, 40, 59, 60, 61, 64, 136
O'Malley, Joe 105, 106
Ó Móráin, Mícheál 34, 38, 40
O'Neill, Barbara 114
O'Neill, Terry 114
O'Neill, Tipp 115
Opperman, Johnny 90
O'Reilly, Dr Tony 3, 5, 7, 104, 105, 106, 114, 127
O'Reilly, Emily 5
O'Rourke, Mary 96, 119, 120, 121
Ó Tuama, Barra 70
Owen, Nora 130

## P

Paircéir, Seamus 135
Patton, Eoin 16, 139

Phelan. Angela 18
Pitcher, Bartle 104, 105
Power, Paddy 68
Power, Seán 68, 92
Purcell, John 22

## R

Reid, Fr Alex 46
Reynolds, Albert 25, 26, 44, 45, 46,
    47, 48, 53, 65, 68, 71, 85, 86,
    91, 92, 95, 96, 102, 113, 116,
    120, 121, 127, 128, 130
Roarty, Michael J. 114
Robinson, Edward G. 146
Robinson, President Mary 71, 95, 146
Rooney, Dan 114
Ryan, Eoin 116
Ryan, Richie 62, 63, 116

## S

Scally, Vincent 76
Shatter, Alan 135
Smith, Michael 85
Smurfit, Michael 127
Smyth, Noel 100, 133, 134
Spanich, Stan 97, 98, 99, 100
Spring, Dick 45
Stakelum, Jack 132
Stephenson, Sam 122
Sullivan, Sergeant Dan 107, 108

Sweetman, Gerard 62, 64

## T

Thatcher, Margaret 22, 28, 111, 144, 145
Thompson, Brian 114
Travers, Garda James 59, 60, 61, 62, 63, 64, 65, 78
Traynor, Des 127, 131, 134, 135, 154
Treacy, Noel 85
Tully, Daniel 114
Tully, Sergeant Tom 101, 109

## W

Walsh, Dick 72
Walsh, John 79
Webster, Max 16, 17, 94
Welch, John 114
Whelan, Ann 22, 24
Whelehan, Harry 94
Williams, Joan 131
Wilson, Harold 121
Wilson, John 106
Wojcik, Denise Marie 99
Woods, Dr Michael 69, 71, 95
Wren, Larry 101
Wright, Ed 97, 98, 99

Printed in Great Britain
by Amazon